Mary's Simple Graces

Messages From The Virgin Mary

Kermie Wohlenhaus, Ph.D. has also authored:

How to Talk and Actually Listen to Your Guardian Angel
The award-winning *Shopping with the Virgin Mary*
Angels in Sacred Texts series which includes:
The Complete Reference to Angels in The Bible
A Quick Reference Guide to Angels in The Bible
The Complete Reference to Angels in The Book of Mormon
The Complete Reference to Angels in The Koran (Qur'an)

Mary's Simple Graces

Messages From The Virgin Mary

Kermie Wohlenhaus, Ph.D.

Kermie & the Angels Press   Tucson, Arizona

All Biblical verses are from the New King James Version of the Bible, used with permission by James Nelson.

To contact the author
Kermie Wohlenhaus
P. O. Box 64282
Tucson, AZ 85728
www.KermieWohlenhaus.com
KermieandtheAngels@gmail.com

This edition was prepared for publication by
Ghost River Images
5350 East Fourth Street
Tucson, Arizona 85711
www.ghostriverimages.com

Front Cover Design by Kermie Wohlenhaus

ISBN: 978-0-9907327-4-7

Library of Congress Control Number: 2017908292

Published in the United States of America
First Edition: June, 2017

Introduction

While writing *Shopping with the Virgin Mary*, I came across a book that, by the title, indicated it contained messages from the Virgin Mary. But upon opening the book, I was disappointed to find only the author's prayers and her *own* thoughts about the Beloved Mother. As I was standing there, with book in hand, I commented to Mary that I have never seen a meditation book directly from her and it would be so helpful for me, and possibly many others, to have her words of hope, love, and comfort. She told me at the time, that someday, I would help her write the exact book I was looking for. I was flattered that she would even think I could be someone to help her write such a book.

Sometime later, though, as I was editing the meditation book story for *Shopping with the Virgin Mary*, my editor looked up at me and said, "Now is the time to write this!" I knew it was true. So I said a prayer, asking for guidance from Mary, and began.

Daily I would sit and write the words Mary spoke to me. For six months I would record what she wanted to say. Then one day Mary stopped and I knew that she was done.

The name *"Mary's Simple Graces"* came when I asked Mary what she wanted to call the book of meditations from her. "Simple Graces," she said, "similar to those I give with my hands, but these are from my heart." I, of course, argued that this title would be confusing and misconstrued as the blessings we say before meals to give thanks. People would think it a book of table graces from Mary. But no matter how much I resisted, the name kept coming to mind, repeating itself over and over again.

By her suggestion, I looked up the word "Graces" in the dictionary, and one of the definitions was actually: "a word coined for the favors granted and answers given by the Virgin Mary." So I gave in and knew it was the perfect title.

This book can be opened to any page for Mary will direct you to just the right grace that will help you that day. You may also start at the beginning, if you wish, and work your way through to the end. As you see, there are no dates on the pages, only Her words – Spirit letters from her to you and me. Even though these passages have been lightly edited for easier reading, both the editor and I have stayed true to her words as I heard them.

May the Divine and Mary's love, light, and grace bless us all.

Kermie

Kermie Wohlenhaus, Ph.D.
www.KermieWohlenhaus.com

Mary's Simple Graces

I am here for each and every one who asks. I will always answer the call. Just ask and then listen with your whole being, and at some time, with perfect timing, you will hear my response. The answer may come from someone else's lips, from a situation a co-worker is sharing with you, you may read an article, or overhear a conversation you recognize as the answer to your prayer. Notice how many ways I am able to talk to you. I am not limited to my voice only.

Do not get disappointed if you seem not to "hear" me. Listen with all your senses and be lightly aware of what is happening around you. I hear your questions and pleas. You are growing in your ability to hear me in *all* the ways I communicate. I love you and send you my love and graces … always.

Mary

The tiredness you feel is your lack of asking me into your life. You are doing so much by yourself. Let me do more of the work while you walk in joy and appreciation. Rest in me, love in me, and allow my power to have its way with all your problems and distractions. You have so much help, if you would only ask *and* allow it to unfold.

Sometimes a situation is unfolding like a blooming flower and you rush its process by prying open the petals – wanting to have the fullness of the bloom too soon. Just as a flower, the beauty of my outcome is fragrant, awe inspiring, and a thing of beauty. But in your impatience and fear that the end result needs your help, you destroy the final grace of what the flower has to offer.

Wait for me to show you the process of the grievance you have given to me. Watch from the sidelines as I teach you the Divine way how a circumstance can slowly proceed and be finalized. You will be amazed at the results. If you will be patient, you will be able to watch the flower blossom. I am with you … always.

Mary

We love you and wish you the best today, whatever you do, we are there. The Divine, the angels, and I want you to know that … always. We will repeat it often. So when you feel so alone, you will hear this phrase in your mind – "We are with you."

Compassion is an action that will soften your heart. It will lower your blood pressure, slow your heart rate, and strengthen your immune system. Many times health care workers will respond to an emergency and work for hours on end. Then they will collapse from exhaustion, but they are happier and healthier than they have ever been. Their compassion, caring, and service helps them live longer and more fulfilled than most.

Ask us to help you be of service and you will activate troops of angels and the power of my heart and love. As you walk even lighter, you will find that miracles occur on a speedy basis. We love to help you be of service to humanity, the Earth, and all the creatures upon her. Love and serve often.

As you serve, remember to serve the body as well. Nourishment, liquids, sleep, rest, and fun will keep the body running smoothly. As your body is built to serve you, you in turn serve it and others.

We are always with you,
Mary

Love and laughter bring spirit closer. Seek enjoyment as you engage in your work. Try out different activities to see if they are fulfilling your fun quotient. Surround yourself with people who laugh, who are grateful, and have a positive outlook on life.

Deep laughter is the best medicine. Just like deep love – it heals –cleaning your aura and energy field of impurities. Laughing shoots out beams of white light that blasts all dark or stale energy out of your field. Negativity breaks down and crumbles to the ground as neutral particles. It is one of the easiest ways to burst the shackles of depression, grayness, and the blahs.

Seek movies, activities, performances, and books that will make you laugh. Find your favorite author, comedian, and sport to bring excitement into your life and you will become energized.

My son, Jesus, was very funny. He was serious about his work, but he loved a good party, and he knew the power of laughter. His work was exhausting but he surrounded himself with friends and loved ones who cherished his company and his wit.

So go in fun, laughter, and joy.
Mary

Joy is what to seek in your day. "What is it that brings me joy?" This is a question to ask yourself as you awaken. If there are responsibilities, work, and duty; find the time to be in joy while doing these necessities. Joy can be carried with you inside.

Find that place quickly upon awakening, by prayer, meditation, and gratitude. Go to joy first; the joy to be alive, to have options, to make choices – all these bring joy.

Finding gratitude for what you have, instead of highlighting what is wrong in the world or your life, is a good way to start your day. You can focus on fixing what needs to be done, but all can be done with an element of a joyful heart if your day began with gratitude and appreciation.

Appreciate the body knowing how wonderful sleep feels, how refreshing waking up to the new day feels, how the warmth of a shower and water raining over your skin feels, and how delicious food tastes, being satisfied and nourished.

Be grateful for the time to read, learn, talk, and relate to others. All are joyful acts. Joy is the core of your being if you let it be and keep it there. Come always from a place of joy, appreciation, and gratitude.

We send joy on wings and prayer. My touch is one of power, love, and joy. Seek my touch often – just ask, I will not deny you.

You are so loved,
Mary

Mary's Simple Graces

Appreciation is a word that all in the spirit world love. We glow with gladness when you thank us for a miracle we performed to help you on your earthly walk. We like to remind you that we are indeed here to support your highest and best good.

We appreciate you for inviting us into your daily lives to co-create with you. We love that you take us to work, to a party, to help you through a trying time, and most of all, when you pray for others; family, friends, the city, state, country, or the world in which you live.

We can do so much more with your permission and invitation. You can receive power by asking, praying, and meditating. When you do, we can also send you love. So pray, say the rosary, and read sacred text often. Meditate and hear our voices. See me and the angels in the world and throughout the times.

You are so loved and we love it when what we do for you is appreciated and acknowledged.

Sending love and wisdom … always,
Mary

Mary's Simple Graces

Fear is a four letter word that you need never say again. To replace it say, "I just don't know what will happen in the future, but I am leaving it in Divine hands of love and all will turn out for the best."

You are never alone with any current or future event or situation. Please listen to me when I say you are never alone, you don't have to only rely on your own resources.

Depend upon the power of God, the power of the Universe, the power of all that is love and light. Trust that all is for your highest and best.

Am I not your Mother? Aren't you under my shield? Yes, you are under my protection and care. All is well. All Is Well! Close your eyes and say, "All is in the Divine's hands, and I am there too."

If you could be aware of just a small fraction of the Divine support you have at your disposal, you would be amazed that you were ever afraid. But, that is why we are invisible – to help strengthen your own faith in the unseen, the future good, and in your own ability to turn it over.

Sleep well, go in peace, and know that you rest in the power of kindness and love.

Mary

Indecision occurs only when you haven't heard the right choice yet. There are so many options for any situation. Look for more roads – ask for more opportunities. Sometimes the mind is stuck on only one or two solutions to a problem and, to you, it may not seem that either is acceptable.

Look and ask for many more ways through your difficulty. You will be surprised that there are so many more paths leading through the deep forest. Some are easier and some are more difficult. Try to remain open to see a better trail.

Sit in silence when all is chaotic until a road opens to you. Sometimes it is a matter of sitting. Wait for the solution to reveal itself. Be patient. The answer will come. The very act of being silent and listening attracts all the possibilities to rush to you and be a part of your journey.

Wait and see. You do not have to act now, let it come to you in your silence and meditation. All is well.

Mary

Rocky river paths are the stepping stones across the rushing current. They are the bridge to the other side. Step only one step at a time, surely, with purpose and diligence. You will reach your goal. Sometimes, it is a matter of only looking at the next possibility, the next sure step, instead of the whole distance which, of course, can be overwhelming, full of fear, and doubt. See the steps that reveal themselves as does a maze, which can only be seen while on the next rock.

Go slowly, deliberately, and with great determination. You will cross. I am cheering you on to the risky but solid step; as a mother encourages a child to first crawl, then to stand, then to step, and eventually to run.

You will learn so much by doing, even though you wish I would just lift you up and place you on the other side of your difficulty. But the skills you need will only be learned by trying it on your own. A parent cannot learn to walk for his or her child. I can only guide you in the process.

So step off. I am here to catch and to put you back on your feet again. You are surrounded by such an abundance of love.

Mary

Mary's Simple Graces

The joy of a frosty glass of water in summer, a warm drink in winter, a cool breeze when it is stifling, and a warm fire on a brisk night – that is my presence to you. Ask for it often in all that you do. Even the simplest tasks will be so much easier with me in them. I want to be with you in all that you do; not just in times of great danger or need. Please ask me to be with you in your work, play, and sleep. I will be there instantly.

My joy is seeing you touched by my love and graces. Your job is to receive with open arms and to surrender to spirit love. I will go where you go. I will serve as you serve others. I will strengthen you as you heal those around you. Use me as a resource often, talk about me often, and ask me to be in your life as much as you can remember. I am with you always, so put me to work.

Mary

The Miraculous Medal and the image on Juan Diego's tilma, called Our Lady of Guadalupe, are both gifts of love and healing for all to have as their own. Please wear the images, hang them around your neck, have them in your home, car, and at work. Have them everywhere to remind you that I have touched you with my healing presence.

Rosaries are for everyone as well. Utilize them in times of need, joy, and worship. The spiritual is getting squeezed out by the distractions of the world: TV, videos, newspapers, magazines, internet, social media, games, and world news. The more you partake in these addictive distractions, the more you will find yourself focused on the physical world instead of the true source of life – the Divine.

Take the time and make the effort to come to me, where your spiritual path leads you. Be in nature, away from the chaos, the energy of the world, and be with me. I am waiting …

Mary

Disease is a disharmony within you that can be healed. It takes an inward look at what caused this dis-harmony and at that point a deep healing begins. Any belief, action, or thought that is not your "true" self may cause disharmony in the body. Anytime you ignore your inner guidance it will find a stronger way to get your attention.

I can heal, but only if you follow my suggestions and guidance. So many times I will ask you to stop a certain behavior and you resist. Out of habit you continue until your disease gets so bad that it can cause you to lose your life. At that point, you are then "cured" and your spirit soars back to Source for healing. You are instantly healed. You will also see clearly what the problem was and what the true cause of the manifestation.

But why wait? Begin now to ask me for healing and listen to my suggestions. I will show you where to go to get your cure. It could be from doctors, healers, counselors, spiritual offerings, but always, always find where you have not been true to yourself. Surrender to the process and all will be well.

Mary

True wealth is a manifestation of your beliefs about your worth. Some feel very rich even though they may not have much money, just as some feel poor, needy, and in fear who are cash wealthy. It is an inner richness that is more important to manifest rather than cash on the physical plane.

Do what you are guided to do after asking me for more money. I will tell you; I see the paths you can take for greater financial gains. It isn't a secret or hidden from you, but sometimes you may be focused on the wrong career or job believing it will bring you the desired outcome. That is not always true. Seek that which brings you inner wealth first.

Follow my lead and I will bring you to true prosperity – inside and out. The outward manifestation of money is quite easy. It is only a matter of finding the path to wealth for each of you. It is custom made and I will help you find that door to your riches. Ask and you shall be led. Seek and you shall find. Listen and you shall hear. Do and you shall manifest.

Mary

Healing of the mind is important since your thoughts are with you everywhere and at all times. Make peace of mind the number one priority of your physical body. To have this harmony of mind, meditate often, walk with me, stay in the moment, talk with me, and most of all, listen to my words.

Your mind will be very busy thinking of ways to be close to me. I am already here. Please do what I have asked of you and there is no longer a need to be in a state of worry, fear, obsession, and resentment. I will show you the way out. You will learn to trust. Trust, faith, and letting it go is the path to sanity.

Sometimes medicine, herbs, and energy work are essential for peace of mind. The mind is chemistry and I will lead you to what you need. After asking, be open to all suggestions that come your way. Many times, I lead through other people. You may happen to read something or see a TV show that reveals the answer you need. Help is all around.

Be of hope and seek your answers, but first start by asking me. Then your seeking will be streamlined for the least effort and it will pull in much synchronicity.

I am with you always, to help. Call on me.
Mary

Mary's Simple Graces

Fun is vital to a happy life. Focus on fun wherever you are. At the job, at home, and everywhere you go. Engage with those you meet in cheerfulness, laughter, joy, and at the very least, with a smile. Some call me the Sorrowful Mother, and yes, life was hard for me at times too. But the joy of life is not to be missed. I laughed often in my life, always astonished by God's grace and love.

Be open to and speak graciously to those around you that are filled with joy. They are the jewels of life; they can shift a mood, heal the body, and place you on a much higher plane.

Love and laughter are the preventative medicines of all time. Sometimes life needs focus and work, but then there is a time to appreciate and rejoice in the completion of the day or project. Do not miss that joy by going onto another project immediately. Stop and appreciate a job well done, and especially, a job that was done with a positive perspective and love.

Mary

Mary's Simple Graces

Bring in the light, shift the darkness of a room, or an event! Shine forth – open the windows – be in the sun – light the fire. There is no need for darkness anymore. There was a time in human history called the "Dark Ages." This time you are living in is actually the "Time of Light." Enlightenment is everywhere. You can see people who are just full of light. Their aura shines and everyone sees and feels them for the outer energy lightens with their inner presence.

Bring light to a wound; illuminate where it is hidden, tucked away; drag it into the open, right on the table – let it breath. Once it is in the open, creative discussion can ensue for the best cure to repair the problem and what was so secretly stashed. Open the blinds, draw back the shutters, and let the light beams dance freely in your lives. I will be with you in this brightness of being.

Yours … Always!
Mary

Mary's Simple Graces

Beauty is all around you even in the most dismal of places. Look for it as a child seeks candy from a jar. Thrust your eyes into the search for great beauty, inside and out. One need only look up to see a lovely sky, sunset, or rain fall. Look out to see the beauty of truth, bravery, and courage. Look within to see the beauty of a heart beat, kindness, and love of self. Seek other beings who show the exclusive elegance of their lives.

See the grace of God, the spirit soaring with each breath you take, the charm of meditation, synchronicity, and the flow of the tides of life. Seek beauty often; she will not elude you; she is there – everywhere – if you will look for her.

Try not to be distracted by that which you judge as less than beautiful, but know it is only a work in process, and see, instead, the beauty of potential and how far it has come. Look in the mirror; see me right beside you, shining on your exquisite self. All is truly beautiful; you will see it if you look.

Mary

What I said to Juan Diego so many years ago still holds true for you today.

"Be not troubled, nor afraid. Am I not here, I, your Mother? Are you not beneath my protection? Am I not your shield?"

Allow me to shield you, to protect you, and to help you as The Holy Mother. Be not afraid or troubled about anything. I am here with you and praying for you always. Use your rosary; lay your burdens into my care; let them go into my hands. I will work wonders in the best way possible. You may not see it at the time, but, eventually, as it unfolds, you will see the blossom of the miracle that is happening.

I will never leave you. I will always be guiding you to the Divine. I love you my children, come to me.

Mary

Mary's Simple Graces

Worship God in all you do. Use my words that I spoke to Elizabeth in praise of the power of the Divine. Listen to them in your hearts as I speak them again:

"My soul magnifies the Almighty, and my spirit rejoices in God my Deliverer. For God has regarded the lowly state of the Divine's maidservant; for behold, from now on all generations will call me blessed. For God who is mighty has done great things for me and holy is God's name. Divine mercy is with those who love God from generation to generation. The Creator has shown strength with a strong arm, scattering the proud in the imagination of their hearts. The Divine has put down the mighty from their thrones, exalted the lowly, filled the hungry with good things, and the rich have been sent away empty."*

You are with me as we magnify the Divine together. Whenever you praise or worship the One, ask me to be with you, and I, and the angels will fill your heart, soul, and mind with love, light, and health. Let us repeat it again, all together now …

Yours Always,
Mary

Inclusive version of Luke 1:46-53

Obsession of the mind – when a situation keeps going over and over in your thoughts, when you can't sleep, when you are distracted from daily tasks, when you become physically clumsy. The only answer is to either come to a resolution, or, if there is nothing you can do about it, now or in the future – let it come to me.

Bring problems and worries to me always, especially, if they are keeping you from doing your best in your everyday life. In order to do that, you could say the rosary and then release them to my care with each bead. Pray that I intercede on your behalf and wish that will be the best for all involved.

Write all on a piece of paper, even if just a word, or journal about the condition and lay it near or under my statue or picture. There is no right nor wrong way; all you really have to do is ask.

Then when the offending thought comes into your mind, remind yourself that you have given it to me and that I am fully capable of handling it. Release the thought with blessings and feel anticipation to see how I will help you with the resolution.

Sometimes, though, you are not able to give me something that you are avoiding due to fear, embarrassment, or procrastination. In that case, ask for my strength to move forward and I will walk with you as you take care of what you need to do. Hand in hand we can do it together.

Remember, I am with you always,
Mary

Fear of not having enough money is polluting the air around you. Clear it with gratitude for all that you do have. You have so much, just look around. People, shelter, transportation, jobs, resources, health, air, water, fire, and the very Earth you stand on. All are worthy of your appreciation. Begin to change the thoughts of fear into overwhelming gratitude for everything you have.

When it is a temptation to worry about what you don't have or more likely, what you may not have at some future date, continue to shift and discipline your mind to focus on your present abundance. If you had food on the table today, remember that others may not be as fortunate. If you can lighten their burden, then please do, but don't do it with a fearful heart. Do it with a grateful heart.

I am here to help with the pivoting of these negative thinking patterns into ones of joy, release, and relief. The future will come and go, and you may be worrying through all of it, unless you begin today to practice the positive, the gratitude, and the delight of that which has graced your life. Joyful, joyful, we adore you.

Mary

This world isn't about getting your way, or getting what you think you want, but in serving in any way possible. The takers of the world are unhappy and alone, seeking always that next item or person they can possess. They are empty most of the time until they again receive their desires, but it is so fleeting and the need becomes larger.

On the other hand, those who give – fulfill their needs on an ongoing basis. They are never left wanting. They sometimes need to learn to receive from others as their abundance grows, but if they humbly accept and appreciate the gifts given, they will be balanced in their inflow and outflow.

If you need more, give more. All worry will disappear as you pray for ways to give what you have. The mind then is trained to look for the ways your gifts can help the world and those around you. It is a fulfilling way to be. You will smile when you lie down at night knowing that a day's work has been worthy of your time and energy. Give, give, and then give some more and watch, accept, and rejoice in what is given to you in return. All is in Divine order. You will know that as you practice these truths.

Mary

Love is an energy that can not be missed or taken lightly. It is a connection between two living beings that exceeds all else. Love is the Divine. There is no more holy essence in the universe. Love all; treat them with respect and kindness then allow them to be who they are.

Can those who abuse your loving ways take advantage of you? Yes, so detach from them, but love them from afar. They especially need it, but not at your expense or your well being. Sometimes, the best one can do is to love someone from a distance. As that person grows (or not), it is best to not put your own life in danger, for self love is also a commandment.

Only you can love yourself to such great depths. As that is happening, you will learn to take care of yourself before taking care of others. Then you will come from a full heart and mind instead of one only partially filled and needy.

If you do not take care of yourself, you will expect someone else to take care of you as you give to the world. This is not good and will cause great difficulties. Give to yourself with love, and then take that core love into the world and share it with others. Caring for self is full of many surprises. Begin that practice early in the morning and you will be set for the day.

With great love,
Mary

Ask for more prosperity and I will give you ideas, insights, and new ways of bringing abundance into your life. It can be fun making money and doesn't have to be difficult. First ask and then listen to where you are led. It will become apparent how to invest, get a promotion, find a new job, invent a product, sell something, or be inspired to numerous ways to create more financial flow.

Creating money is easy when following inspired action. Ask, then go forth and observe as ideas break into your sleep or meditation. Great thoughts also occur while you are having fun.

The universe is abundant and wanting to teach you how to let go of limiting thoughts and how to step forward into a new economic level. Feel it right now. What would it feel like to have greater wealth? Ask for it, feel it, and expect it. The flow is a constant. It is ever changing – in and out – around – continuously upwards, or falling away. You get to choose financial abundance and then magnetize it into your energy field. You will be so amazed at how easy it is to create a different money reality. Try it, you won't be disappointed.

Mary

Love is in the air, all around it swirls. Breathe it in. It is such a gift to acknowledge and celebrate love. Romantic love is the icing on the cake of life – to find new love is intoxicating. Allow it to bake, follow it into the depths of a soul, and surrender to its beckoning call of true bliss. It will fling up your darkest shadow to be healed in the light of love; it will trample your selfishness and break any limitations in personality. But most of all it will introduce you to the Divine in a heart-opening-blast.

Love often, love deeply, and love well. Follow your longing to find your inner lover again. The knowledge learned from love is forever nestled in the soul. The Universal wisdom of love will inform those who venture into it for the first time. Love is never, ever wrong – ever. Even if your heart gets broken, love had a purpose for you.

My love for you, my children, is the deepest when you are in pain and lost. My love will find you because you have been cracked open to allow the subtleness and flame of the Divine Mother's love to penetrate your inner world. Rest in love; bask in its light and brightness; and create using the excess of love's radiant pulse.

I love you always,
Mary

Courage is knowingly going into a difficult situation. When you do, take me, the Divine, and your awakened self with you. It is walking through fear; it is a growth experience. The more courage you exhibit now, the more you will risk the next time.

Bravery is courage in action; to be of service, to do the right action in the face of great consequence. Those of courage, those of bravery, those of action, know themselves and their failings all too well. Their weakness becomes their strength. They know their inner battles and overcome them in the face of truth and love.

Be of courage … take brave and inspired action. Take me with you as you face your fears, your opponents, and enemies. The risk is worth the effort, for great acts of courage lead us, always, to greater leaps of faith, social and inner change.

Mary

Sleep well tonight with prayers of gratitude for a day of richness overflowing with life. Let go of any negative judgment you may hold about an event or person. Give it all to me for the evening and let me hold it in my gentle arms. As I watch over you tonight, feel my hand running lovingly through your hair, gentle kisses on your cheek, filling your heart with warmth and tenderness.

Sleep, my child, for I am with you always, softening dreams, protecting you from stress and worry. You are underneath my shield protected from life's storms, resting in my sweet grace. Allow your body to restore itself in deep slumber. I am your Mother, rocking you on a cloud of love.

Mary

You will find a partner when you love yourself so much that you no longer need it, because the energy of need repulses the energy of love. The energy of need attracts only those who are needy too. When you are dependent on others to fulfill your love bucket, you attract those who also have a less than a full love container and you both have very little to offer; only a lot to take.

When you continue to make a concerted effort to let go of fear, focus on faith, enjoy your own company, love yourself, and feel emotionally stable – then, and only then, will you attract a different type of lover. At that point, you will feel a deeper kind of love that you didn't even know existed.

Two independent self-loving people will attract to themselves the same and be amazed at the possibility of such expansive caring. So look within yourself to meet your greatest lover. I will always help and give suggestions on how to nurture self and you will be very happy doing it as your self-love will grow and grow and grow. Love is always here for you.

The simple intimacy from that one special person is instinctual and is a basic human desire. So do your work to be happy within yourself, have fun with you, care for you, and love on you. Your perfect partner will be right around the corner once you have this love of self firmly in place.

Walking in Divine love and light,
Mary

Mary's Simple Graces

If you continue to look and focus on what health you don't have, or what things you don't possess, or are always looking for more, more, more – you will never have enough. Have enough now and not only that, but see how abundant you are right in this moment! Being rich is seeing what all you do have. Even the wealthiest person can be poor if she or he looks only at what others who are wealthier have that she or he does not possess.

Love, use, and enjoy all that you have right in this moment. You will be the richest person you will ever know all the time. Say: "I am the richest person I will ever know" and see where that will take you.

Money is an energy that will be attracted to those who love it and enjoy what joy it has bought in the past or present. Love all that it brings to you, even the simplest pleasures; the cool drink, the meal, a sweet dessert, gas for the car, and where that vehicle has taken you. List all of your appreciations all day long and see how much you grow in abundance. It is flowing to you; gratitude will bring you ever so much more.

Mary

You are on the physical plane so you will know the difference between love and hate, good and evil, fear and faith, and health and disease. You are able to choose which attribute you want to live and experience how it feels in your body. It is an opportunity for you to observe so many feelings, choices, and the consequences of your actions based on your beliefs.

You will also find great relief when you turn to the more positive choices – love and faith. It is quite phenomenal the amount of knowledge there is to learn. I am here to help you with your choices … if you wish.

Many want to put their own opinions onto someone else's situation, but you will find that your experiences can help only you. Until someone is ready to hear what wisdom you have to share, you may as well utilize your own breath to push the clouds across the sky.

Only when others are ready will they open their hearts at the right time to hear your wisdom on any given subject. You are all very unique and have your own path to travel. So go with grace, love, and support as this Earth school challenges you with many remarkable opportunities.

Always with great love,
Mary

The Universe – Creation is as big as a thought can travel. It is expanding each moment and is beyond human comprehension. It is important to stay focused on this world, but for a true perspective, embrace the vastness of this entire dimension. Even though it is so enormous, I am always with you while you are here on your Earthly journey.

I touch your hand, have your back, and am by your side every step of the way. You can feel me as you turn to see who is behind you – it is I. I go wherever you go and watch as you courageously step out of your comfort zone into the world of risk and faith. Miracles happen when you are expanding your realm, adventuring out to learn more, be more, and do more.

So as you allow yourselves to expand, the energy of reaching will generate its own support for you. Feel that uplifting love carry you to your next resting place. Always then … rest in me.

Yours,
Mary

Today was a job well done. You followed my guidance with smooth synchronicity – open always for the unexpected and my subtle leading. Thank you, for it is a joy to work with you – even if you do not feel like I am communicating with you and it is only your imagination. You are still committed to follow through and do it anyway.

Someday, when you need it most, I will be there louder, but for now, as you continue to learn about my gentle ways of encouraging you through your minutes, hours and days, my voice is becoming more familiar.

Go now to bed and sleep with the slumber of the weary. I will protect you in the night and gently whisper you awake in the morning. Good night, my dear.

Mary

When you find yourself with no real schedule, no clear direction, just step forth in Good Orderly Direction (GOD). If you find yourself just sitting around eating, watching TV, playing video games, or being bored, get into action in whatever needs to be done next. It could be washing clothes, going to the grocery store, or calling a friend in need. Do something that has good motive and purpose rather than filling up the space with unhealthy food, mindless entertainment, or self-centered thoughts that do not bring forth happiness and health.

Cooking a meal that will nourish you and those around you, gardening, cleaning house or walking the dog – all will bring a richness of living life on those days that will draw you out of a negative frame of mind. Remember, there is always time for reflection, meditation, and prayer – always time to read spiritual writings that uplift and strengthen.

So on those rainy days, the blue days, take some action that will turn this around. Press reset – begin with gratitude and find simple actions that blossom into a joy filled day.

Mary

Eating healthy, nourishing food will bring a new life force to your body and senses. Saying a small prayer before consuming your meal adds the spiritual into what is entering your body in a way that goes to every cell – blessing it with energy and vitality.

Praying during the preparation of sustaining nourishment mixes Divine intention with the flavors and love for those who consume the fare. If you could only see with your physical eyes what a difference cooking with intention makes, you would weep that you haven't done it for every meal from the day you could put pot to fire.

But now you know, so remember to make your kitchen and garden a sanctuary of love and blessing. Ask the Divine to be there and ask me to join you in the loving task of culinary creation. We will respond in kind and bless you for the asking and in the doing.

Mary

Cleaning house is a sacred rite. As you fluff the energetics of your surroundings, set the intention of peace, health, and tranquility with every sweep of the mop, dust cloth, and rag. All is well in your home when swabbed with love, light, and prayer. Chant or sing while cleaning and see what a difference that makes. Put on spiritual music, dance in each room, thanking it for holding you and yours safe and protected. The house and home holds great relaxation and healing for those who enter when the occupant spruces up the energy on a regular basis.

Push out the dust, dirt, and grime asking it to carry off the particles of energy that are no longer useful. Let go of the old. Perfume with incense, oils, or essences to sanctify the space as holy. Ask for the light of the Divine and angels to fill each room. Ask me to be with you each step you take as you exorcize the negative and renew with the bright and cheery. I love to clean with you.

Cleaning my house brought me such joy when I would put flowers in the corners, fill the water pots, and air out the rugs. Having a home that is pleasing each time you enter is the one blessing that is available to all on a daily basis. Don't let this joy slip by in the mundane of daily living. Take up your cloth, open the doors, and let the sun shine in.

Lovingly,
Mary

Mary's Simple Graces

To have broken items around creates a crack that allows the positive energy to drain away. Repair, throw out, or get rid of those things that are not working in their proper manner or damaged. If you acquire an object that you can fix, do it quickly and enjoy how it serves you. It will bring such joy for only a small price. It becomes a treasure. But once it has lost its usefulness, move it out of your living space so it does not create clutter and accumulate injured thoughts.

Move anything and everything out that is no longer serving you. If you tire of it or it is too old to be of use, give it to someone who will bring it back into service. Restore the flow in your life and home; renew food stuffs, utensils, linens, and books that linger way past their time. Bless them and send them out the door.

Give old items new tasks in the yard or in a different room. Move the furniture every so often. No longer tolerate stale energy or old, stuffy furniture. Rejoice in the fresh new objects of your desire. Breathe in the change of life.

Mary

Study often, read something, or take a class to exercise the brain. Repeating the same mental activity over and over again will drain your energy. Many want to "dull the brain" with addictive actions. But I am saying that bringing in new adventures, people, and thoughts will activate the mind, allowing it to expand and remain healthy. Change your point of view every so often taking on a differing perspective just to see how it feels. Listen to someone intently to hear what they are truly saying, ask questions for clarification, and delve into what knowledge they have to share.

Experience new lands, ways of travel, climates, or cultures – watch movies of experiences not your own – immerse yourself into a novel place. Look, listen, and feel the difference and see how it will forever add a broader view. Travel often to foreign pockets of diverse culture, even within the same city or country where you live. Just get out more to expand your life and experience.

Mary

The spiritual realm is home for your soul. Visit often. Take the time to allow your soul to be fed and your heart to beat in time with the great rhythm of the universe. Fill your lungs with limitless expansion as if standing on the edge of a vast vista. Allow your consciousness the freedom to explore and to feel once more the freedom of merging with the Divine.

I live in this domain of unconditional love and vastness. Joy fills my every cell. My sorrow comes from seeing you get bogged down with the harshness of your everyday existence when within and above you is the freedom you crave. Drink in the gift of creation, the dimensional pool of glittering life. Drink it into your physical body and bask in the central sun that has only warmth for your soul and will not burn.

You are so loved from so many other dimensions, ever encouraging you upwards. We are here for you whenever you call or come to meet us. We are full of light, love, and help that is practical and will make your existence on the planet more fulfilling and rich. We love you always.

Mary

Whenever you look to the future and try to predict outcomes, you leave God and the magic of spirit out of the equation. Future events tend to be looked at through the lenses of fear. Looking ahead is a way for the mind to prepare for the upcoming disasters, not to calm the mind with the tranquility of the synchronicity it can't possibly predict.

Call me into all events that are ongoing and then go forward into the time and, as it unfolds, you will see me instead of the visioned horrors that the imagination can tell you about in such grand detail. I will never leave you and as you ask for my intercession, you will be surprised how each situation will shift in ways that will only be for the benefit of all concerned.

Call on me now for all uncertain endings. Call me often to calm your mind and strengthen your faith that all is, indeed, in Divine order.

Mary

Physical and mental exercise is very important to the body, the mind, and spiritual growth. Come to me those who are heavy laden. It works to lay it all down at my feet too and allow me to shower your burden and you with everlasting graces. I am so pleased when you bring me that which is too cumbersome and allow me to help in my way.

Continue to offer it all to me and exercise your faith and belief that all will be well and in fact, better than even before. It is hard to let go of and not try to manage something when there is so much fear, but the absolute best thing you can do is to release it to a Higher Power. That power can be me, the Divine, or any being that you pray to.

I am gentle in my dealings, as a mother can be, with unconditional love and delight in your ways. So please bring it all to me and I will take it to the Divine for the greatest Power in the Universe to infuse with love.

Mary

Aah, love in the afternoon. Love in the springtime; love in the winter; love in the summer; all the seasons are grand for love. When two people find each other and a spark is ignited, there is nothing like it in the whole world. What we see from the other dimension is a very large firework display, as seen in some of your celebrations. It is just like that. A large beam of light comes forth from the two persons and blasts through the heavens into the Universe. It is quite attractive and we all love to see this originating from the Earth.

Whenever you fall in love, whenever you choose love over hatred, whenever an unselfish act of love is put forth, this same gigantic firework show bursts through the heavy density of your physical plane. It adds so much light and when it is put together with all the other love comets happening around the world, the Earth looks like a huge round, pincushion of light. We bathe in this light and it adds to the possibility of more love emerging from you and those around you. So love well, love deeply, and love often.

With much love,
Mary

Cleansing your homes, cars, furniture, and bodies often releases the negative energy that has accumulated. So many times as you travel in the world, you pick up a dense vibration from other people and things you encounter. Wash your body and your hair each day to release this from your own field. Wash your hands and feet when you would like to shift and move into a more positive perspective.

The waters of the Earth are the best for this deep cleansing. By pouring spring fed waters – even bottled spring water – over your body, your energy field will be enhanced and brightened.

Drinking waters of the Earth or rain water from the heavens, cleanse the cells of your body, bathing your outer and inner self. As the water enters your blood stream, it cleanses all it touches and replenishes cells to bring an added gift of Earthen blessing. Drink well, drink deeply, and let it flow to and through you so it can be returned back to the Earth.

Mary

Acquisition is addicting and can clutter your living spaces. Too much stuff calls for more storage, drains energy, and becomes a burden of responsibility to gas up, plug in, and maintain. I too loved to feel fine fabrics, was attracted to the sparkle of jewels and the comfort of luxury, but knew that it came at a price. As the rabbi taught – keep your treasures in heaven instead of on the Earth where others will be attracted to them and want to steal, covet, or become jealous; too high of a price for me. Try to keep it simple.

I had quality clothing but not much of it. As I have been teaching you, go for quality not quantity. That way there is fluidity of items coming in and out as you need and use them. If you store them away, they can deteriorate, lose their usefulness, and become a waste of your time, energy, and space. So limit yourself to a few necessary possessions that you love.

With much love,
Mary

Laughter is so much fun. Please seek out places, movies, books, and people who create laughter. There are comedy clubs to attend, TV shows, and people who strike your funny bone. Watch, read, and listen to them often. Laughter is healing; humor is contagious; even a smile will lighten your and someone else's day.

I laugh too, at the way the Divine works. It is so much fun to see what seems to be a major obstacle, turn into a series of enlightening situations that bring lightheartedness to the experience.

Practice laughing; open your mouth and show those teeth. Once in a while, an artist will paint me laughing or smiling. What a joy it is to see my shift from the sorrowful to the laughing Virgin. I did smile and laugh much in my life on Earth. Much was difficult, but there was so much that brought me joy. So go have fun, laugh, love, and be healthy.

Mary

Natural disaster happens. It is such a part of nature to cleanse, reshape, and stretch out a bit. She loves to unfold and yawn, relieving areas that have just gotten tight around her belt. But, unfortunately, when she lets go, those creatures and plants living upon her are damaged or destroyed. Watch where you put your homes, she has wrinkles for a reason. It is obvious where she has moved and broken loose before, so be mindful that you are living upon a living entity.

Some think that it is a great tragedy when the Earth shifts, but in all actuality, she has always done this. Your great scientists have predicted her moves and have called out warnings to you. Heed their knowledge. Even though the property may have a wonderful view, if it is on a fault line, your house may be swallowed up if you build there.

Waters of the oceans are extremely powerful. When they churn and are disturbed, they are relentless to those living on the shores. Know this and be wise in your decisions. You, of course, can ignore these warnings, but do not act as if this is a great freakish disaster. You knew and chose to live in danger. Those who live on shaky ground, need to always have their running shoes on so they can move quickly when the Earth begins to tremble.

Mary

Political and spiritual leaders who are chosen by the people are given a chance to be servants instead of rulers. Be wise in your choice. Be not fooled by the glitz and pomp. Look for good, solid, active, serving leaders. Ones who merely sit on a throne in greed and glory will be thrown out. Those who know how to serve will be loved and all are blessed.

Sometimes wealth and prestige are what attract the vote. This is not what will serve the nation's daily needs. Yes, the wealthy are great to look at, read about, and dream of meeting someday, but they sometimes are selfish people, who are only looking for their own ambitions of power and money.

Those who give of themselves in many different ways are the best. They may not always be the ones that have the spotlight or microphone, but they do have everyone's heart. Vote for them. They will not let you down. It is hard to discern these from the rest, but look at their track records, the fruits of their labors. Go seek them out and place them on the stage, illuminate their successes and applaud them, then vote them into office. You will never be sorry for such a choice.

Mary

Career is the focus of your life's work. It is where you can make a living being of service to others in the way that is unique, using your skills, talents, and passions. Finding your life work is easy for some and difficult for others. Sometimes a job will teach you the skills that are needed for your career in the future. If you are at a workplace that is not your passion, look for the opportunities it has to offer, then focus on those. Learn all you can, then move on.

Your career is about you and what you can offer the world through joy. There will never be another you, so equip yourself with all the tools, mentors, and education you will need to be the best at what you do. Ask me, the Divine, all your guides and angels for help. Then your work will be placed on a higher plane and the power of synchronicity, strength, and magic will open and sustain you as your strive to improve your service.

Go forth now, blessed with my grace, the grace of God, and the power of the Universe to add your unique offering to the world.

Mary

Mary's Simple Graces

Partnering is a very complex relationship. It can happen in so many ways. Sometimes there is an instant recognition that this is the one. Often, though, there is a shopping around for the one who is a mutual fit. When you meet those people who partner with you, whether it is in a business, a personal relationship, or a project of some sort, honor that person for enhancing what you are both trying to do.

When a want and need goes forth from your heart, another soul or two will be drawn energetically to that call. A series of very specific events will occur that will bring you two (or three or more) together. There will be a meeting, a connection, and it will be as if a miracle has happened for all involved. As the relationship develops, enthusiasm will build as the visions expand, are talked about, and planned.

Honor and appreciate these connections. They are so important as something strong and beautiful is being built.

Mary

Negative emotions are an indication that something needs attention. When it is fear or anger you may choose to run, avoid, or walk through it with faith and courage. Then you can either keep it silently to yourself or join in grand celebrations! Emotions are the body's barometer and usually require the spotlight or action of some sort.

When negative emotions are denied, they manifest in a physical malady or they may be expressed inappropriately. In the case of anger, it may not be safe to rant at the situation or person that has caused the anger. The anger may be held or vented in a safer environment. If it is not allowed to have safe expression, though, it may fester and be released on an innocent person or thing. But nevertheless, all emotions are to be felt and dealt with on some level and as soon as possible.

Emotions are not to be feared. Some go to great lengths to keep their living situations calm, quiet, and in harmony. They work so much to maintain this calm that they will not enter into relationships, avoid work issues, and supress their emotions with food, drink, drugs and/or smoke. There is a better way. Feel and deal. Talk about them; find out why they cropped up.

Learning about the inner workings of your emotions is vital to good mental health. Seek out those who counsel and help with these confusing state of feelings. Seek me and I will give you strength to go forth and do the work necessary for peace of mind and health.

Mary

Mary's Simple Graces

Being outside is one of the best healing techniques that is offered on this Earth. Be out in nature often, feel her sunlight on your face, the breeze in your hair, see the beauty of her creation. Breathe in the clean, cool air and fill your lungs with life giving oxygen. Air and water are the two most important ingredients for the human body. Without those two, the life force will leave and death occurs. Drink water and breath to your heart's content. Both are flowing through the body carrying nourishment and removing waste.

Fill your lungs with your breath and bring in light with each inhale. When exhaling see the used and exchanged energy go forth into the universe. Drink clean water, blessing it as you drink and when you eliminate, thank your organs for working so well to keep you healthy.

In spirit I do not have the physical apparatus to exchange toxins with renewable sources. It is different. What I have now is the pulsing of the Divine, the energy of love and a finer light entering my light body, cleansing, and uplifting. Surrounded by love, it is easy to stay close to Source. It is exalting to be in this dimension.

Know there is much to learn on the physical plane and one of the most important teaching is to create harmony within the body. Do this with water, air, and being in natural places.

Mary

Mary's Simple Graces

Glory Be! Be filled with wonder and tremendous love for the power of the Divine. The Creator is so good, generous, and kind. Not like the God of yore, where all was damnation and punishment. No, God is a Good God – loving, understanding, and always, always encouraging us to be who we were created to be and to live into our potential.

We are asked to be our very best. Seek the highest choice in all you do. That does not mean that you have to have multiple jobs, be over responsible, never allowing yourself a break – always giving, giving, giving. No, it is about harmony, balance – giving to others as you give to yourself.

Would you work your friend to a frazzle and never give them a break? Then do not do it to yourself. Do unto you as you would do unto others that you love. This is the great lesson for some. Others may have a different lesson. Be kind to others as you are kind to yourself and loved ones. Be filled with compassion, drop the selfishness, stay open to the joy of giving and receiving.

Some people are so afraid to love, themselves or others, so to them I say – take a chance. You cannot break free of fear by sitting in it. Walk through it; expand to add trust into the world. Trust those who are trustworthy. Do not lavish trust on those who have shown they are incapable of holding a trust. Avoid them, pray for them, and seek the solid, the salt of the Earth. They are all around you. Open to them and you will have true friendships.

Mary

Sing praises of joy, of happiness, of unconditional love. All is changing and the best, absolute best way through a changing time is with prayer and gratitude. In fact, change the gratitude to extreme praise. Extremely praise your situation, the good that is in it. Even with the death of a loved one or great loss, people and love show up in unexpected ways. Extremely praise them and those that led them to you in your hour of need.

If there is a health issue, thank that knee or stomach for all the work it has done so far and for the good job it has done in keeping everything in order. Thank it for the warning, the ache, and the pain bringing your attention to it to begin healing and listen deeply for the message it has to offer. Maybe your troubled body parts are providing you with an important lesson, acting on your behalf, or ushering you into a softer life.

Slow down, eat more nutritious food, or exercise in a different way. It is all praise worthy. So lift up your hearts to all goodness in time of crisis. It is everywhere if you step out of the bog of worry and rise above it to gain the higher perspective of the good that is present. Praise often, praise loudly, and praise well.

Mary

Sleep is the body's way of renewal. Dreaming is the mind and soul's playground for loosening up the day-to-day structure and allowing great freedom of imagination. The soul will travel to exotic places in dreamland. The mind is free to think whatever it wishes. There is no conscious mind structuring your thoughts about daily needs, problem solving, memory, or communication. It is wild and free to wander with abandon. The soul and mind are quietly opening the doors of freedom so as not to wake the conscious mind from its slumber.

The human spirit plays in the safety of the higher dimensions. Sometimes it studies a problem that you may have gone to bed with and goes seeking consul from wiser beings. Sometimes it creates, so when you awaken, the new project unfolds easily. Dreaming is a magical time for the mind … ever giving it permission to flow where it wants, drifting here and there slowly, quietly, and with great joy. Sleep well tonight, sleep well.

Mary

Companionship is very important to the human heart, whether it is a partner, friend, pet, or being of light. The need to have someone who will bond with you is a human need. So it is wise to surround yourself with people who will be in highest harmony with your essence. Many have a pack of party friends or special interest friends who will accompany them when doing certain activities they enjoy. But get a soul mate friend, one who is of your essence, who "gets you" – one that words are almost unnecessary.

Keep your friendships active, don't allow them to lapse. Just a phone call to say you are thinking of them or an email/text keeps the bonds fresh. This will keep the connection from corroding and withering. Send some love to those you value, especially in busy times. Send love to all you know, keeping the pathway open from your heart to theirs.

I am sending love, my heart is always open,
Mary

Wise counsel is an important resource. I am one of your wise counselors. Use me often. I am readily available to you in times of need or just to share about a situation or your day. I love to hear from you and give you encouragement, assistance, and counsel. I am always here.

Wise counsel with mentors and spiritual advisors is very important too. Choose wisely those you go to for advice, private conversations, and who you trust so deeply. Honor those people and what they do. They may be your lawyer, teacher, doctor, pastor, or therapist – all honorable professionals who have a great commitment to confidentiality. Use them as well. Do not wait until it is dire; use them to prevent a crisis, when you get an inkling that something is amiss. Call them, set up an appointment, see if they have time to hear you out and confer what your next step could be. You have wise human confidants and a universe full of Divine beings ready to help … if you but call.

Pray often and seek meditative counsel. We are all here for you. It will be easier if you step out of isolation with a problem and share it with us or someone on the physical plane. We all love you … you are not alone.

Mary

When you make yourself go to work, you are making a choice to exchange your time and talents for money. You can shift your attitude so that you are going to be of service, no matter what you do. How can I be of best service for those hours I am at my job? Great question to ask on your commute. Who can I help? What can I do to help myself, to learn, to meet those who will advance me in some way to be of better service?

Employment has many levels aside from the money aspect. You are given what you call benefits – use them, especially educational benefits. These will greatly improve your skills and therefore your paycheck. Utilize all continuing education benefits, also. Likewise, use your health insurance to take care of your body with your annual teeth cleanings, exams, and all you need to do to maintain health and productivity.

Take your time off and go places that will enhance your life and have an adventure. Where do you want to visit and take in the local color? Go, plan, and find interesting aspects of this world you live in. Traveling, having fun, taking time off, are just as important as the money that provides food for your table and shelter for your body.

Look at your career as an opportunity to be of service to others and to enhance your life and joy. There is so much that is provided for you and so much to receive and give.

Mary

Judgment can suck the wind right out of you. Once you judge someone harshly, you can never go back to the original innocent view of them. Now you have made a decision whether to like them or not.

Discernment can be useful, though, in evaluating if you would like to be in a deeper relationship with someone, whether it is a co-worker, friend, intimate partner, or even service provider. Testing to see if a person is trust worthy is vital. When you have to relate with a professional in a dependent way, as you would a surgeon or caregiver, your judgment helps you to see them clearly and to make decisions on how to best interact with them. Ask questions, see what answers they provide.

Discrimination can be used in a positive way for discernment or it can either be used to hurt people or judge them. If used in a negative way it can be quite destructive to you and to them. Remember, you may become your judgments, so judge softly, quietly, and with love. Know in your heart what you believe about something or someone. When appropriate, be open to change, to adjust your opinion.

Let it all go to the universe and bless everyone and every situation. This will only bring good to you and to others. You may learn that you were wrong in your assessment. Ask for guidance for right decisions and understanding based on love and wisdom. I am always here to help.

Mary

Pain in a body part is difficult to handle, no matter where it is. When pain is acute, the body screams out "EMERGENCY!" All nerves are firing and flight or fight stress is on full blast. The only way to deal with it is to change the source of pain – then distract the pain with medication or a nerve block. The same is true with pain in the mind.

Once the source is discovered and dealt with, the healing can begin. It is time to numb the pain in any way that will not cause more damage. But look at healing the source as well as decreasing the symptoms.

Those who have chronic pain are the bravest of all. They daily have to fight a battle within their bodies and still live life. Let them know how courageous you think they are with their daily struggle. Dealing with so much pain is not for the weary or the weak. It can create strength in even the weakest or a giving up. Go forth and be in relief, be grateful and remember what it was like to live and work in such pain.

Mary

Mary's Simple Graces

Coming home again after a long journey is like walking into a safe, secure, and cozy heart-filled sanctuary. Gratitude for where you live is crystal clear for a few days after such an absence. We see the old familiar as new again and actually enjoy the broken-in-feeling.

Before you leave on your next vacation adventure, clean the house from top to bottom so when you return you will bring in the new energy you accumulated on your travels. When you open your luggage to unload treasures, they will be welcome in their new environment and there will actually be an energy shift that expands the existing level.

So go on the road often, leave for small or long increments of time, just know that when you finally cross your threshold again, you will be welcomed and cocooned into your own harmonious space.

I am home too, come to me often and feel the presence of love.

Mary

Luxury has its price. As you reach to higher and higher levels of want and ownership, along comes the responsibility and culture of that level. Those who play in the lifestyle of wealth have tremendous pressure to keep pace with their peers, always striving for the better, bigger, and the best that money can buy.

The "millionaire next door" though, the one who is a working class wealthy person, is down home and sidesteps these trappings of bigger is better. This class owns what they need and has a rich lifestyle without the pressure from others. They peer with their co-workers and their families who helped them acquire such wealth. They tend to play, party, and hang out with these co-creators of their wealth. That way they are admired as they share the products of their wealth with those who will enjoy it with them without vying for the biggest and best. Their quality comes in the form of good, solid fun.

Seek this level first, and then make a choice if you wish to play where there is a higher level of competition among the celebrities, royals, wealthy business owners, and athletes. Even some of these wish only to be with their roots and have much happier, richer lives. Then they will die leaving money to their descendents and not just to the designers.

Mary

Eat well; eat nourishing food. Yes, I talk about this often so you remember it. Feed your body 3-5 times a day. Always ask for and pick the healthy choice.

Drink cool refreshing water. Allow the flow to go in and through in a cleansing fashion. Bless all that comes in and thank all as it goes out carrying toxins from the body.

All is a cycle, in and out, flowing around and through. The air you breathe is cleansing, bringing in life force, smells, pollen, moisture, and spirit. Breath deeply, then let go as it is released again, taking with it that which is no longer needed.

Breathe, eat, and drink are all life sustaining and vital to human life. Treat the vessel your soul embodies well and it will work well for you. Then, when you let it go at the end of life, the passing will be a thankful transition from the physical to the spiritual with gratitude for a vessel well nurtured and no longer needed. It will be proud to have served your soul well. Serve it and it will serve you.

Mary

When you are off balance, your body or mind will create a crisis so there is a pendulum swing to the other side to offset the imbalance. If one works too hard and has no time to rest, an illness may present itself so there is plenty of time to rest.

If there is too much excess in any area of your life, the opposite will rush in to adjust the inequality. This is the natural process. See it in nature, even in the driest climates, floods will come wash away the dust and replace it with small plants who wait for such a time. Fires burn the forest, but then pop open seed containers releasing the beginnings for new growth to find its way.

So as you schedule your lives, plan to balance work and rest. Work, rest, play, movement, creativity, spirituality, nourishment, refreshment, and sleep all need their time. If not, then there will be a counter movement to give you abundance of such essential elements for a healthy existence.

Love is the only element that is not balanced with hate. One is able to live a completely loving life without the adverse effects of its opposite. Love often, love more, and love completely.

Mary

Holidays are important to remember and embrace. Thanksgiving gives pause for gratitude, Christmas for giving, Veteran's Day for remembering the price of freedom, and Valentine's Day for love. Celebrate and contemplate traditional and non-traditional holy days of all peoples. You live in a diverse culture and you can participate in all religious and non-religious festivities. All have a richness honed by time and a collective energy that rolls over and accumulates from year to year. Ride the wave of each holiday as you will for its vitality will bless you and yours.

The New Year is one of the most important times, for it is a new beginning. All cultures have a new start time marking the close of one chapter and the start of another. It is a jumping off place into the sea of possibilities. Leap with determination and anticipation into the fresh potential of the rest of your life. Re-invent yourself, your dreams, and your way of living. It is your time to focus on what you want next and appreciate what you have accomplished. Upon the foundation of the past – the new will be built. Dream it well and then act with conviction. Believe it fully – all is yours.

Mary

Simplicity is the key to wealth. If one defines wealth as a certain amount of money, it will be difficult to obtain. But if one knows that wealth is in the richness of the life led, the beauty that surrounds, the love that is given, and the opportunity that is taken, with appreciation, then the bar for a wealthy life is obtainable daily.

Ask the wealthy if they are happy. They are if they appreciate and have much freedom with their money. But not if they still have fear of something being taken, or the constant envy of those who have more.

If the rich are always acquiring instead of enjoying what they have, there will not be the immense pleasure and freedom received from so much money, as you may think. So, an abundance of money isn't always a factor in the happiness of the wealthy. But the rich abundance of safety, love, gratitude, giving, receiving, and freedom is worth all the effort it takes to create such manifestation.

My richness I give freely to you for I know that as I give, much more is returned to me.

Yours always,
Mary

Harvest is a time of rest, of appreciation, and a time of abundance from all the labor that has gone on before. Sit back, enjoy, share what you have gained from your hard work and know that you did well. Celebration of a job well done is in order, so lay back and sigh from what you learned and accomplished. I am proud of you for all the work rendered.

This is the time of year of completion, of high honors, of graduation. It is a time to close one door and to heal, slow down, and be at peace. The new has not yet started and it won't until you are ready to hit the ground running again. You know how to win the race, but do you know how to accept the trophy and praise? To rest after? Learn to do that, open yourself to the acclaims of others and the prize. Know that you have completed an amazing performance. Then rest in appreciation, for all is well, all is complete.

Mary

Mary's Simple Graces

The rising of the sun brings the dawn of a new day. Each day is a new beginning. A fresh start, open to creation, ask what you want on this daily canvas. It is yours, treat it well, and go forth with anticipation and wonder as the morning and minutes unfold. Make it fresh like new paint over dingy walls; blow out the old and open the curtains of this bright future.

Leave the past in the past, stay in this moment. This is the only day you have that can be changed, heightened, and molded. Use this day wisely, for it truly is the first step to the rest of your life.

The choices you make in this day create the foundation of your tomorrows. Tend to the basics, the sturdiness, and sound construction to hold the strong structure for as long as you need it. I am here with you in the now, the building of this day. Talk to me often, ask for advice, and let me show you the vision of possibilities. Together we can reach the highest potential for you and others to best optimize a life worth living.

I am always here for you and everyone who asks,
Mary

Space is the stuff between mass. It is the air, the atmosphere surrounding the Universe, the planets, stars, and heavenly bodies. To get a glimpse of creation, just look up, especially into the starry night. With the blue sky of day, there seems to be a lid on the Earth, but in the darkness of night, the blue ceiling exposes her secrets.

Vast is the Universe, thus, vast is the Creator. Incomprehensible is what we call Source Energy, the Divine, or God/dess. When viewed from the evening sky, consciousness expands to meet the echo of space. Go there often – into the silent and immense openness. You are under my wing, in my heart, and protected by my shield. So go freely about in the Universe, enjoying all of creation. It is yours and mine – our home for the soul.

Mary

Silent Night, Holy Night. It was an amazing night for Joseph and I. The pain of child birth was hard, it being my first time having a baby and being away from my home and family. But it did make Joseph and I closer. We had many hardships. We could not go back home for many years. We weren't prepared to go into Egypt, but we did survive. Friends and family took care of the house and property for us. They all understood and were glad that we and the baby survived. It was a terrible time for many families with young children who were killed by the soldiers carrying out orders – a horrible decree for the infants, families, and the soldiers alike.

Jesus was a miracle child, as you know. The events around his birth were truly miraculous; the angels, the wise men, and the shepherds – all surprisingly unexpected and full of joy, pointing to the working of God in our lives. We were well taken care of by the Divine and the angels. Never since have there been such events for us. I will hold that time in my heart forever.

Merry Christmas to the world; peace, goodwill, and love to all.

Forever your Mother,
Mary

Motherhood holds great responsibility. As you ask for my motherly care, I immediately come into your presence. You are mine to care for and to guide home to the Divine. Ask me to be with you in this life of challenges and opportunities. Some are so lost in this world. Just ask and I will come to even the darkest and most lost soul who has given up all hope.

Please come. Ask. See what happens after you change and rest in my arms. I will protect and lead you out of even the densest forest of madness and gloom. I will never fail you. It may not be in the way you think I will or should come to you, but it will be the best way.

Then remember as you climb out of the well, that I am here to walk with you, not only in emergencies, but in your daily life, to consult and recommend the best path and decision. You always have free choice, but there is one who can give you solid and right advice. It is me. Asking is all that is required.

Forever here,
Mary

Love is a many splendid thing but you can make it more confusing than necessary. Actually, you do not have to do anything to allow love in your life. Just open your heart, give as you want, and receive from the same fountain. It is not something that has to be figured out. The most powerful energy in the world, planet, and universe is love. It is what holds everything together, and it will find its own place, connecting itself where it desires.

There is no manipulating of love; either it is or it is not. Someone does not have to do anything for love to appear; it finds you on its own time. So relax into love; lay back as it arrives to you. And if it finds you worthy, follow it, let it lead you to your destiny.

The Divine energy is pure love so how can love be anything but Divine? You can complicate it all you want, but just as water finds its way, so will love. Let it guide you to where you need to be

Believe me, you will know when it calls to you. Just follow it with nothing but good intentions. Honor it, be grateful for it, and know that you will eventually sleep, eat, and be in harmony when it has had its way with you.

Loving you,
Mary

Play is vital for good health, wealth, and spiritual growth. Play allows the mind to expand, the body to move, and you to enjoy something that is purely uplifting. Sometimes there is a limit to how much frolic you allow yourself before you whip yourself back into shape and make yourself go back to work. But then your work is forced. So I say – make your career a passion for joy while making money. It is a blessing to do that, for you and for others. If your work isn't what you would call "fun", whose job is it to make it more lighthearted? Your boss? Your customers? No, it is your job to laugh and have some pleasure. All will appreciate it.

If there was no play in the world, nothing would be invented. Inventions usually come from creative play. So laugh, stay upbeat, and have a variety of pleasurable activities surrounding you. You don't need much to enjoy yourself, it is mostly an attitude.

You could have a great deal of fun and not let anyone know just what a good time you are actually having. Just go about your work with liveliness within. You can look just as dull as all the rest of your co-workers, but inside you are having the time of your life. Try it sometime when all is boring and tedious, just have fun inside, practice the joy in all you do, lighten up and you will never be the same again.

Mary

Selfishness is an interesting word. It can mean that one is focused on self for the betterment of their work, service, and what can be given to the world. It can also be the overwhelming greed and need for time, money, and/or love. Selfishness can also be the inability to look beyond self and, therefore, have no interest, or even awareness of others. This selfishness has no compassion, empathy, or caring whatsoever. This is the selfishness that causes great suffering for the person and those around her or him.

The selfishness that turns the focus on improvement or the expansion of self, one's potential for the good of creativity, knowledge, or health is a very good use of this self-enhancing trait. For ultimately, this use and extreme narrowing of energy to achieve one's goals will enable all of us to expand and appreciate one's devotion to their art. Sometimes great musicians, artists, or brilliant minds will neglect all but their "work" and because of this sacrifice, all of us benefit.

So weigh these definitions of selfishness when someone you love calls you "selfish". Which one is it that fits what you are doing? Is it extreme passion for your "work" and calling in life, or is it the demand for all things to revolve and be given to you?

Even those who have contributed greatly in life could be considered as selfish to those they love, since most of their time and energy was on their contributions to the world. Their efforts are truly blessed. But focused attention on individual needs and wants, overriding the universal goodwill of others, drains life force from the many to enhance the wants of the one. See which calling of self is yours, the self focus to give or the self focus to get.

Always giving,
Mary

Blessing those around you is vital for it brings the light to the darkness that some people live in. When you drive by a homeless person or someone who seems to need extra help, bless them and ask for Divine blessings to come upon them. All blessings come back to you as well, even though that is not the primary intention. Blessings can not attract the fruit of hatred, misunderstanding, or depression. It will only enlighten the one who blesses as well as the blessed.

If you knew how important blessing was, you would do it without ceasing. A prayer for others will strengthen their hope and resolve to get through whatever they need to walk through.

Help one another, bless often, silently, or even in the spoken word. When parting, a simple "Bless you!" will put Divine flow into someone's day and life. Bless more and see love return to your heart.

Blessing you,
Mary

I am the Immaculate Conception. Think about those words, how powerful they are. You are my children, thus, you also are the daughters and sons of The Immaculate Conception. You are as pure, as full of light, and as loved by the Divine as I am. You are powerful beings of light within a physical body. Once your body deteriorates and dies, you will return to your glorious light body with all the joys of a student returning home after graduation – a job well done.

I will be there to greet and welcome you back home. Your new knowledge and soul's evolution will look so good on you. It will beam all the way through the door into heaven. You will arrive on a stream of light and with cheers of the angels and loved ones. All will know that the battle, the honors, and the recognition have been won.

Remember this in the hard times: they are only temporary, as temporary as your time on Earth. You will be home with me again soon. Until then, learn your lessons well, step out into your potential and sleep peacefully knowing that I am here with you, always, during your earthen journey.

Mary

Family includes those with whom you live, those who brought you into the world, and also those who your soul recognizes as spiritual family. I am your spiritual family. Those ties are very strong and the recognition deep. It goes beyond conscious mind and can only be known as an inner knowing and loving. Your heart will open and you will know that a beloved person has entered into your life, a love that goes beyond the time you currently live.

Family members bring important support to you in this lifetime. You choose to be there for the gifts they give for your soul mission. Even if it is a difficult family life, it has strengthened you and given you aspects you need later in life. Open your heart to these people/soul family members, allow them to speak their truths, and then go on.

I am your soul mother, sending my love and support as you go forth from this day. Open to *my* graces and you will be lifted up to higher perspectives of joy, hope, and love.

Forever yours,
Mary

Seek your Divine Source often, daily, by the minute, and live in God's presence – singing songs of joy and prayer. Then listen to the silence – it is filled with God's voice. The Divine has much to say about everything, but oh, so few listen.

Hear the birds singing praise, the grass as it grows higher to the sky, the clouds as they drift by, all have their own sounds. The mountains have a song as clear as the whales do. But who sits and listens to them and their ancient wisdom? Some do and those who have, hear beyond the words of the people; they hear as Creation and the Creator speak. The heart-beat of the Universe is their heartbeat.

Dance to the Divine music in a sacred place. Listen more, not to people, even though they have stories to tell … but listen to God. Communicate often and build a relationship of trust and love. I will help you if you ask.

Mary

Mary's Simple Graces

Welcome home little one, the angels and I are here to be with you today. Your home is your daily talk with us. We love it when you take the time to sit down to have a chat, to listen, to feel, and be in our presence. We love you so much.

Now, be sure to smell the roses, as you say, today. I love my roses, so fragrant and sweet. Their beauty lasts in my heart and I love to give them to all I adore.

Look for the roses wherever you are. See if they don't lift your spirit and calm your mind. Roses have such powerful healing abilities. We know so little about them. Go to them often and you will find me there in the midst of them too.

Breathe in rose fragrance, feel the softness of their petals, notice the fine point of their thorns. See how roses flourish after being pruned so very far back and then bud profusely in the spring. Know roses as I know them – in all their many ways. Then turn and view all of creation in this holy and luscious way.

Mary

Peace is a prayer for all to pray. War is against all that is life. Love is the answer; hatred is the disease. Pray for peace, love, and life. You will learn more and more as time goes on. As a community of nations, the brightest will come to terms and teach the others about peace and what that looks like from within to without. Those who are not peaceful in their spirits can only bring disharmony into their world.

Pray for them, that all may know and live in peace. As the pendulum swings, it will eventually land on this harmonious place, but only after much strife. It is truly in letting go of fear that one can find peace – simple, but not easy to do.

You would think that banning fear from within would be a joyous act, but many feel that if there is no fear, they would be inert; unable to do any purposeful work. Not true. When fear is banished, the perfect work, the perfect love, and your perfect body will be automatically drawn to your spirit. It is so.

Mary

A marriage exists when two or more people are drawn together to form a bond, a focused direction to build something into the world. A marriage can be between co-workers, students, lovers, husband and wife, spouses, partners, or friends. As marriage is redefined in the various cultures, one can see that marriage is happening in so many ways to the delight of those within such bonds.

The common good is paramount and the parts of the marriage work together to compliment each other's skill. This will benefit both and allow success to come to all. It is a powerful unit that finds each other for the focused purpose.

When you find such a person or group, step forward bravely and take your place within this marriage. Know that it is a blessing that you found each other and that the journey will be supported by those around you. Go forth in commitment, communication, and trust.

All is indeed well.
Mary

When you find yourself down in the dumps, or having the blues, think about what you can do to find purpose with living. Try a new adventure, new friends, a trip, or something that will expand your energetic life. Once negativity sets in, it is hard to shift, but being outside in nature will help.

Clinical depression is another matter and may need the help of a professional and possibly medication. No shame in that; there are many reasons for this chemical imbalance. It could be hormones, food choices, brain chemistry, hereditary, or past trauma, just to name a few. But for those everyday blahs, there are many choices to improve that energy. In fact, it is best not to entertain these blue thoughts and feelings; they pave certain pathways that will deepen if allowed to continue for long.

Besides being in nature, try being of service to someone, looking for a new perspective, find humor, eat healthy nutrition, meditate, pray, or do creative activities – all will enlighten your spirit. Helping others may be one of the most effective ways to change the blues and put you in the pink again. There is nothing like volunteering to keep retired persons from their own mental obsession of self. Being with others in a way that brings joy or service will take the edge off your own dull feelings.

I am always here for you too. Bring all your cares to me and I will put into motion events that will lift you onto a higher plane. We all have our sorrows.

Many of you have even called me the Sorrowful Mother. But I didn't have to stay in such sorrow. It really was short lived as the extreme, Divine joy of resurrection replaced my deepest sadness. It did save the world.

Mary

Mary's Simple Graces

It is so important to be "out of doors" often. Breathe deeply the clean air of life. Hear the birds in the trees and bushes. All is well in the world with the sun on your face and the Earth beneath your feet. Bathe in the waters, eat from the fruits, nuts, and vegetables. Pick them right off the vines and trees. All is in order for your health and vitality if you take the time and partake.

Move about on the Earth. Walk everyday and feel the rain, the snow, the wind, the warmth, the bitter cold. All is exclusively here on this planet. No where else has the same beauty. We are blessed to have been born on this planet. The Divine has created it for your pleasure, health, and growth. Seek and enjoy all there is in life. It will not last forever.

Mary

All is well. Say it often, "All is well." "ALL is well," "All IS well," "All is WELL," "ALL IS WELL!" For it is, my children, All is Well. When judgement is placed upon happenings in your life, it seems like it must be bad, or wrong, or it could be better, say instead … "All is well!"

From my perspective, yes, there is much that can be improved and let me tell you, it is improving. When a situation arises that points out that something is wrong, it needs to be fixed and then, again, all will be well.

There is constant change in the world. Everything is evolving. Change is inevitable. So allow the change to happen – go with it – augment it and then sail down the river again. Without rapids, there is no flow. The rapids speed our growth and accelerate the change that must occur. Embrace it as a good thing. Then you too will say often, "All is Well!"

Mary

Many times physical problems are created to slow you down and to turn you in a direction you have been dreaming about. For instance, many will create colds and flu to provide the chance to lay around and rest more, to watch TV, read, or just get out of the stress of a job. It is a healing time and even though it will interrupt your daily routine, it is always there to serve you.

Look for the gift in every physical problem. Tell that sore knee, "Thank You," for it is letting you know that it is time to focus on healing, possibly through love, therapy, medication, a brace, or even surgery. It is a good thing to finally say, "This is enough, I need to do something about this."

Pain is a touchstone to healing. When in pain, you are unable to ignore the difficulty, work through, or deny it. You have to stop and reevaluate the situation and seek help immediately. Otherwise, you would just let it get worse until your leg falls off. Then you would be without an important component of your motion and this would not be good.

So when your body lets you know that something is amiss, take action quickly. Get your healing going in the right direction so you can get back on track and, hopefully, with a bit more balance in your life, you can step forward again.

Always.
Mary

Hunger for spiritual growth and for the Divine is the most awesome feeling, because you will always be fed. The Divine cannot deny you access to its loving presence. Seek, beg, petition, and inquire often for Divine presence. It will come. It has to. It cannot resist.

Ask early in the morning, upon awakening, for Divine grace, presence, and direction for your day. It will be a glorious day, even with challenges. The request you made at the dawn of your morning will sustain you with synchronicity and provide you with much more ease. You will want to remember to seek God to enter your day and activities.

Some wait until there is a crisis to ask. I advise you to ask now, ask often, and ask with love in your heart. Remember to praise often as the Divine is lit up with love when one appreciates the flow of life and the sacred touch in all dealings. So ask, notice, and express gratitude every day and enjoy a life beyond your wildest dreams.

Mary

Mary's Simple Graces

Running waters of the Earth, growing trees, and shining stars are there for your spiritual nourishment. Visit these with open arms and hearts. As the energy of these forces enter, close the door behind them, oh, so slowly, and breathe in that stored energy until you are in tune with the powerful elements again.

The same with me – call on me; be in my presence and draw me close so I can feed you when you do not feel me as much as you would like. I am always there for you – I never move. Sometimes the clamor of the world will mask my love, but no matter, just as day light masks the stars, they are always there. So it is with me. I love you, I am your mother, friend, and savioress.

Showering you with graces from now unto eternity,
Mary

Friendships are a gift you give yourself. They are your family of choice. They go on with their lives as you continue with yours. But when you meet again, it is a refreshing encounter. Hug and converse often, for human support is so needed. Value your friendships and be there for one another. Blessed is love, and the love of friends is one of the most blessed of all.

I am your friend too; one that will never relocate to a different town to follow a job or spouse. I am the one for you. Go and come at your will, I will be there to share your joys and sorrows. Your love is my love, your challenges are mine too. I will partner with all your travels in this life and beyond. The angels light the way for you and to me. Follow the light. Follow the light back home.

Always!
Mary

If there is nothing you can do about a situation, please bring it to me. I will take it to the highest level of solution for you and shake the foundations so you don't have to. It is easy for me for I see the best possible outcome in all situations and can begin to activate their solutions immediately.

So rest easy next time … no worries … no fretting, not one thing is accomplished by these fearful thoughts. Only prayer and following inspired action can overcome the impossible. Go now and choose … worry or faith. It isn't as easy as it seems, but the outcome and journey to the end is so much better with the faith choice.

Faithfully yours always,
Mary

Mary's Simple Graces

When troubles come, and they always will, pretend that I am standing right next to you. I am holding your hand or you are embraced in my cloak, looking out through my love to the world. It isn't easy to be in this world with so many pitfalls, but they can all be leapt over with a light heart and a knowing that I am with you.

Go slowly into this world of chaos, step gingerly as if in a post-war, land-mine field. I will go ahead and identify the triggers, the trappings to avoid. But you have to keep your eyes on me and not the so called troubles that surround you. I can only keep you safe if you follow my lead and my warnings. But then at the end of the danger, you will know that all is well with me as the guide, the scout. I will never let you down.

Mary

Writing is a disciplined action. But it is truly simple: sit down and write. Put fingers around pen, pen to paper, or, turn on the machine and place your fingers on the keys. Then fill up the blank paper or screen with little forms that make up the words that convey your thoughts.

Write everyday even when you do not feel like it. There will be days that it will be a battle to sit and place fingers on the keys. Likewise, there will be days that you think you are glued to the computer because it is so joyful and fun to see what comes out next.

The same with art; get in that studio and create something. Play, dance, paint, sculpt, and allow the muse to take hold of your body as you create something that has never been envisioned. Watch it flow from you like light from an open spotlight, illuminating the next idea or form.

All is well with your places of inspiration. All it takes is for you to go through that door into your creative mind and spit out what has been rattling around inside of you for so long. Take the chance and sit down, or stand up, and begin. I will be with you.

Mary

Mary's Simple Graces

Put your feet up and relax for it is the day the Lord has made, rejoice and be glad in it. Too much work and not enough appreciation of your labor will make your soul tired. Relax more. Sit and watch the world around you from your back porch. Don't read, write, or play games, just sit and watch.

Notice the birds in their daily flights back and forth in the trees. Observe what new plants you can find that you have never seen before. Travel into the crevices of your yard with your mind's eye. What is under that rock over there?

Observe the visitors to your yard that you rarely notice: squirrels, robins, doves, bees, ants, an assortment of bugs, cats, hawks, raindrops, snowflakes, blowing leaves, debris from the neighborhood – all there to entertain you. Take notice and hear the messages they all have to offer.

I too visit your sanctuaries of house and yard as you invite me. Some have fountains, statues, and small shrines to me. I visit these places often. Some have prayed to me in their home and I have followed their petitions to the residence of the plea. My energy lingers long after the miracle has happened. I can go easily now for the path has been blazed. It is as easy as a wink … I am there. Pray often … I will come.

Mary

The sea is close to the cycles of all. Ebbing and flowing, in and out, spiraling around the Earth. Under the surface water is a flow that moves as a mighty river around the Earth that is not seen from the shore. The shore only offers the wave movement. One has to look and explore deeper to know the true journey of the water.

What once was the water of one coast can become the waters of another coast in a matter of time. All is in motion, you are in motion. Ever changing, ever evolving.

The Earth herself is growing, expanding, and giving birth. Many are so busy upon her that they are sometimes shocked to realize that the dirt they stand on is a live being. She is slow to move, but when she does, there can be a mighty rumble.

The sky is moving as well. Air, particles, moisture, all are rushing by in natural timing. When looking up at the night sky, see the vastness of the Universe and know that the Earth is kind to those upon her and will feed, shelter, and heal everyone. But occasionally, she has to yawn and stretch with growing pains. Allow her to do so… but get out of the way.

Mary

Drink more water. You are dry as a bone and liquids, especially water, moisten the cells of your body and more importantly, your brain. When in dry climates, the air will demand that all around feed the atmosphere with their moisture. To replenish this environmental demand for water, drink often. Sips are fine instead of large amounts. The excess will be drained quickly. Your plumbing will love you for keeping it flowing and detoxified. Your entire body will appreciate the care you are giving it for having chosen to live in such dry climates.

Taking baths or showers will cleanse the outside, while drinking will keep the inside from building toxins and maintain vitality for the new. You have heard many times that spiritual waters of life wash over the soul, rinsing any impurity. It is true to avail yourselves of all the Divine has to offer. Jump in … the water is fine.

Mary

Mary's Simple Graces

Hello Dear Ones – God, angels, Christ, and I are all here waiting for you to connect with us. We are so proud of you and all you do to be of service to this planet and those upon her. You have a special service to offer. Everyone does. It is important to find your special gift and then give it to as many people as you can. It may be to educate, it may be to heal, maybe to entertain. Find what you love to do and that is your service – your addition to life. Do not judge it, just do it again and again ... and again. You will perfect your talent and it will lead you to the next step automatically.

You do not even have to plan the outcomes or peek into the future. You will probably be wrong anyway. Just allow your joy to lead you to the next step, the next lily in the pond. But be sure to rest, relax, pray, and contact your spiritual helpers who have much to say, much to give. They will synchronize events, persons, and the tools you need to accomplish your work. All is indeed in Divine order. Please keep doing what you love to do, it will lead you to your bliss.

Mary

The change of seasons brings in a new enthusiasm to all on the planet. The waiting for winter to end heightens the joy of spring. The heat of summer brings anticipation for the first cooling snowfall. The leaves changing and dropping, the sprouting of that first green shoot through the frosty soil, as each cycle ends, providing joy to all who wait for the next beautiful season.

Also, your change of season brings a growth that cannot be matched – the life journey of infancy, toddler, child, teenager, young adult, adulthood, middle age, through to aging, and finally to death. All have such gifts to offer. As the ocean tides rolls out leaving pools teaming with life which are now exposed, as the clouds pass and the sun warms the Earth, new awakenings and sights are present as never before.

See your life not as going downhill, or closer to death and disease, but look at the tide going out and exposing what was living abundantly just under the surface. Your life has stages, seasons, and a natural rhythm that is not to be missed or covered up with the newest anti-aging product. It is to be shown bravely that aging is something to look forward to, to invest in, to cherish.

Old age is a time of great wisdom, relaxation, and appreciation of a life well lived. It is not over, only a new chapter has appeared. Live this day as if it is your first and the last. Then each accumulated day will add up to a mound, a sea, and a bud of hope for the next phase.

With much love,
Mary

Mary's Simple Graces

Family can be such a foundational learning place. Sometimes, though, family can teach us how not to be, what not to do when you are become parent, spouse, or sibling. The trouble is, you may only realize that in adulthood, when you try your parent's same techniques of raising children that they need to be altered in some way to be more successful. Parenting has to be customized to each child. One way will work for one child and, because of the unique personalities involved, won't work for the other child. There are, however, some basic values that are important for all children to learn and the parent is the most important teacher for these life lessons.

Teachers are also valuable instructors for molding young minds. But as technology brings forth so much information, most learning is now done on-line, through video games, apps, at the movies, or on computers. Children have the opportunity to learn at a faster rate with such advanced educational tools. However, the flip-side to that is they will be exposed to a variety of information that may skew or confuse their growing minds.

You and your children may see more negative images than positive and think the world as a tough, fearful, or scary place. It isn't so. There is more positive happening in this world than negative. It appears differently because the negative gets more "press" and attention.

The negative is ever present in video games, news feeds, and media. Please turn this around, parents. It is important for the children of the world to see that good happens more often than bad. Teach them. Talk to them about it at your mealtime and whenever you are together. Force the negative off the air and replace it with more uplifting stories. It is up to you.

Since you, as adults, create and support the current reality, you have more power to change your world perspective than you think. There will continue to be depression, stress, violence, and suicides until you wake up and change this view of reality for yourselves and your children. You can do this, we will help you. It is your world to make what you want it to be. Heaven or Hell on Earth, you choose.

Mary

When tragedy happens, a wave of love and peace is generated by those who feel empathy and compassion. It is as if a warm, cozy, pink blanket is wrapped around those that are affected by the crisis. The hearts of people are joined to cocoon and comfort the afflicted. The outrage and anger of what has occurred also helps to motivate change so it will never happen again. This binds you as well, knowing you are all in this together.

So much of the time, your focus is on your own lives, families, friends, and work that it is easy to isolate from others. But when a great injustice occurs, people rally and make it right and fair again.

From my perspective, this is a wonderful process to see the compassion from so many. It actually lights up the world with love and this light grid is not penetrable by negative forces. If you could see what this heart passion produces, you would want to find a way to maintain this shield by merely generating more charity for your fellow human family. Unconditional love will win the day.

As you step forth into grief from the effects of any social disease, remember that if the sickness isn't brought forth into the light, the cure cannot be found.

Always the healer,
Mary

Mary's Simple Graces

Yes, some people today do not have the values that were so important in times past. Some are sloppy and seeking only fun and pleasure. They have been taught that their comfort is paramount and they feel entitled to have effortless jobs, relationships, and life. The trouble is, they are heading down a very difficult road, seeking the wrong goals, and, will soon be wondering what went wrong. They do not know how to do the hard work to make ends meet and to live a life of integrity. They only seek the easy way out.

It would be best for you to avoid these morally challenged types and to find those who are efficient in life and competent at their jobs. Befriend them and honor them with appreciation. These folks are invaluable as friends. Seek them out in life and at work. Ask yourself, who is the most caring, detailed, and giving person here? Thank them often for their contribution in your life. Be generous and be grateful for them.

It isn't always the ones who have the looks, money, or flash that we need in our lives. Rather, it is the ones who are solid, faithful, and have deep values that can bring us joy. They know how to share and will perform charitable works. They surround themselves with loving thoughts, turning always toward the honest and true decision each and every time.

Mary

Keep Holy Days (holidays) Holy. Do this by riding the wave of what the holiday is about. July 4th is about freedom; Christmas is about giving and love; Thanksgiving about being grateful; and New Years about new beginnings and starting fresh again.

The holidays that are more commercial also have an angel, a strong guiding force, that takes the highest potential of it and shines Divine light. So Halloween is a holiday of dressing up, candy, and darkness. But it is also a time to be your wild self, to have fun, and to give, give, give – candy, sweets, and playing with dress up.

So on a holiday, take the spiritual theme and use it for your spiritual benefit. Accent the positive. Celebrate it for the day or week and ride that holiday energetic wave to shore as long as you can hang onto your balance. Many are celebrating with you and that will add to your own personal growth and enhance the experience.

Remember my birthday, my day of ascension, my feast days, and those that religion has bestowed upon me. It is a blessed day for me in that so many will observe it in my honor. Catch that wave also. Be with me in all the different ways there are and I will be with you.

Always,
Mary

It is easy to see what others need to do to improve and change their lives. But it is not so easy to be so insightful regarding or make the necessary changes for your own growth. TV, movies, internet, the written word – all have stories to tell about how others live their lives – sometimes real and sometimes fantasy. You, the observer, is the invisible other. Giving you an opportunity, on a regular basis with your media, to learn how others are able to live through certain situations. It may inform you of wise and courageous choices.

If the cameras were turned on you and the authors were to write your story, you would have much to say about what could be changed for the better. You can give yourself this gift right now. Pretend to sit yourself across the table from yourself and listen to how your day went. Listen to the truth about your relationships, career choices, physical body, and spiritual health. What would you advise yourself to do? Then make a decision, a commitment to take your own wise advice. Put a plan in place, set goals, take a risk. See life expand.

Then when you are listening to another's tales of living, loving, and healing, you will have your own truth to share in a very compassionate way. You will share their joys, sorrows, and challenges, as well as offer strong, deeply reflective help.

Know yourself first. Take the beam out of your own eye first and foremost – then and only then, go help the ones who are asking for your perspective. And above all, I am always there for you and love you deeply.

Mary

Mary's Simple Graces

Money, money, money, is on the minds of so many. Make a game out of creating money. See how much money you can make in a given month. Just as you may play a game out of seeing how much weight you can lose in 30 days, see how much you can receive or even save in that amount of time. Put it on paper.

If you go through a mall and do not spend much money, but would have if the clothing fit better, the jewelry was on sale, or the shoes were the right style, then put that down on your register. What did you save for not buying all those items? A wise man said once, "A penny saved is a penny earned." So you just earned a bag of money when you didn't buy anything. Count it.

When you count the money you didn't spend and record it for a month, you will feel so abundant. But don't expect to see that money in your savings account for awhile. You may like this game so much that you may continue to play well into the future, and, you will feel wealthy for all that you saved and tallied.

Money is indeed an energy that normally has much fear attached to it. Consciously attach abundance to it as well as joy and happiness. Hoard it for awhile and see how it changes your view of money. Bless it when you spend it on groceries, gas, and other necessities. The blessing will touch all who come in contact with that particular bill. Spend and give as you want, both consciously and with gratitude.

Pick up money from the ground, even if it is just a penny. It is the universe saying that money is indeed everywhere for you to effortlessly receive and to own. Rejoice in the freedom that your money offers.

I am sending money unexpectedly to you now. Watch for it.

Love,
Mary

When you need to get out, see something new, travel, go on an adventure, or just take a different way to work, what you are seeking is a new perspective and freedom. You have been in a rut, as you call it, doing the same thing over and over again until you are bored with the routine. Routine is good structure and an important stabilizing force, but when it is so repetitive that there is no life left in it, it is time for a change. You can do it now! You don't have to wait for that vacation in a few months – go on vacation now. Even if it is for a weekend.

What does vacation give you? Vacation offers the opportunity to do new activities, meet new people, see new things. Is there any reason this cannot be done right now or within the next 24 hours? Look in the paper or on the internet. See what weird activity you have never attended, go to a different grocery store – a bit out of town, in a suburb, or the next county. Take a chance on meeting people you don't know well in a different department at work. Go to a new church, synagogue, or spiritual center – even out of your own belief system.

Immerse yourself in a book about a different country or dimension. Rent a fancy car and be a tourist in your own home town for the weekend. You will save much by staying in your own bed each night, but plan an itinerary of museums, art shows, concerts, hiking, or attractions you have always wanted to see but never have. Call up friends and ask them over, or better yet, find out what they are doing and tag along. Take day trips or spend the night in a large city close by so the drive time is within a couple hours but you feel you are in a totally different environment.

In other words, find freedom again. It can happen here and now if you just commit to enriching your life. It is good to go to familiar restaurants, see old friends, and have a dependable work situation, but sometimes a new adventure in nature, visiting a park, or sitting by the water is just what the Divine ordered to breathe fresh air into the staleness of your routine.

Mary

Spiritual growth has received a bad name, with the belief that one can only grow through pain and suffering. If one is only able to evolve by taking a "hit" and surrendering to the fire, so be it. But I am here to tell you there is a more loving and gentle way to find the face of God. It is by seeking to be in God's presence and having heart-felt communication with the Divine daily. Ponder that. Seeking presence is by being still; being open to receiving and being willing to spend sometime in silence. To have conversation is to talk and then to listen to the messages, the inner voice, and to pay attention to where your thoughts are led.

Talk to God often, silently or aloud, and know that what you say is always, always, heard. Prayers are answered, but perhaps not in the way you expect. Instead, they are answered in a better way, the highest way for all concerned. Look back on your life. See where prayer was answered in amazing ways. You are never shunned or ignored by the Divine. All requests for spiritual guidance, knowledge, and help are answered and lovingly offered – in Divine timing.

Meditation is listening, waiting, allowing, and staying open to the message wherever it is offered. Sometimes it will have to repeat itself if we miss it the first time, but it will keep trying to get our attention until we accept it as from the Divine. Then, when we turn to accomplish what we are guided to do, we will feel the power, the inspired flow of energy run through us to resolve the situation.

The answer may be different than what you had in mind, but it will always be for your, and all concerned, highest good. Just believe that. When you pray to God or me, we will always, always, give the best help for any and all problems. Remember to follow the guidance with a simple thank you, then we know that you have indeed allowed the goodness into your lives. We only love you!

Mary

Take the time to be with me, walk with me, sit with me, and pray with me. The Rosary is a tool to bring you closer to me. It doesn't matter how many times you say it, or if you say it right. It is about being in my presence and love.

Pray to God more, as if you are talking unceasingly as you walk about life, taking care of your daily responsibilities. In crisis, it is easy to come to us with your problems. But in times of harmony, remember to commune with us with as much fervor as you would when the world is pressing all around you.

We are always there and will offer power and grace in all you do. Try to come often or your spiritually starved soul will create troubles just so you will stop and be with us to feel our comfort, love, and peace again. Then you will admonish yourself for not taking the time to be in our presence and drifting away over and over.

Again, we say, "Stay with us." Make us your home no matter where you are in the world. Even going to the grocery store or to work, go with us firmly and solidly in your heart. We are here, always here. Stay close.

Mary

Mary's Simple Graces

Feed your body, your mind, and also your soul well. Take the time to ask your spirit, "What can I do today to nourish you?" It will readily tell you if you but ask. You could be urged to go for a walk, pet a puppy, or send an email to someone you love. Whatever it is, it is always good advice when the soul is consulted.

Take a chance and ask your soul for your soul mate, for the job that is in harmony with you, the home your soul desires, and the people who delight your spirit. You will be surprised at the wisdom and goodness that will come. Your essence will call forth all it needs once it has permission to do so. It actually will seem effortless to shift anything and everything so as to be in harmony and love with your inner spiritual being.

Take care of the vehicle your soul inhabits in this lifetime; ask how to heal it and keep it disease free. Your spirit is connected with your Higher Power and the universal wisdom. It knows everything and is only waiting for you to prioritize feeding your soul rather than trying to satisfy the never ending ego or desires of the physical plane.

It is exhausting to continue to strive to fulfill all the wants of the mind, thinking it is what will bring peace. No, it is in providing for the desires of the *soul* that will give so much more and will continue throughout eternity. I am here to help.

Mary

Follow your intuition or inspired action. It will take you to the most amazing places. You will get a little nudge to go somewhere that probably isn't on your docket or to do list. But it will keep coming to mind over and over again. No matter what you do, you cannot quiet this small, persistent voice within when there is a need for you to do something or other.

It may ask you to accomplish something that you do not want to do and have been avoiding for quite some time. Like doing your taxes, going to the doctor, or paying off a debt. It may be a fun request such as calling a longtime friend, going to a particular store, or seeing a movie that just keeps coming into mind. Whatever it is, follow this inner guidance and actually go, see, and do what has been in your consciousness.

You will never know unless you act on this inspiration and trust that the message you are receiving is important. It is significant that the Divine will play the message over and over until you give in and actually step forward towards its request. No matter how small, just put one step in front of the other to see what all the fuss is about.

I will only guide you if you ask for my direction and care. It is your choice to listen and do what I am sending you.

Loving you always,
Mary

Friends are important in that they will be there for you in some ways that family will not. Friends share similar interests and there is a lot of fun to be had together. Many times when illness or adversity comes, it is the friends and not the family who step forward to offer a helping hand.

Friendships can last for years as confidants – partners in common goals. Many times friends are of the same age so they can relate to the life stages each of you experience or bonding in an important event that results in a connection that will last a life time.

Honor and support your friends. They are vital for your journey through life's experiences as your soul's family members. Show up for your friends; be there when they need help; show them the kindness that you enjoy when you were the one needing help. Raise a glass with them in celebrations, joys, hold them close when they are in grief and sorrow. Be a confidant witnessing and giving thoughtful and honest advise.

Treat your friendships with gratitude and love. These special loved ones will possibly last far longer than family ties. Cherish the miracle of such unconditional love.

Sending love to you and your beloved friends,
Mary

Parties are gatherings for a mutual celebration. Have fun and enjoy the camaraderie of these interesting people you have called into your life. Meet all you can, picking out the ones that bring you joy. They open worlds that you are not aware of and find those who have passion, energy, positive outlook, and giving hearts.

Bring me along. I love a good party. Remember, I was the one at the Canna wedding feast that asked my son to change the water into wine to continue the celebration. Yes, it was to benefit the host who would not be embarrassed for not providing enough wine for his guests, but it was also to continue the jovial atmosphere. There was so much love in that place.

So don't think that I am only pious and calm in such realms. No, I love to be surrounded by gaiety, music, love, and laughter. I am always there to bring the occasion to a higher level. Bring me along and old arguments, resentments, or family quarrels will be amazingly resolved.

Information will be passed to those who need it through conversation and new connections will be made. Know that I will add the holy to any gathering, whether sacred or not. Once I am called into *any* place, I bring blessings and all *will* be in Divine order.

Mary

Once you know your passion, make a commitment to do that no matter what. Even if you take a break to rest, you will always drift back to it. You will notice that the universe did not take a break and that you will be farther along once you return to your life's work. The momentum of efforts made doing your soul's mission will continue for some time after you have finished for the day, night, week, month, or year. You can pick it up anytime and keep going.

But, be aware that you will not be truly happy unless you are doing what you came here to do. If you are swayed by more money to do something else, or taking on a different career, or putting your time and effort into what you think you "should" be doing, it will be only a tin drum, tinkling in the wind with no real substance for your spirit. Once you turn toward your life's goal, the desire of your heart, *then* you will have much joy and success.

Do not worry that you do not have enough time to complete what you came into life to accomplish. It truly is all a journey. You may not get there in one lifetime, but will have all of eternity to complete your service to the Universe.

So relax, effortlessly ease into your life's work. Have more fun with it, enjoy it, and see where it takes you. This is the right use of your life. You will not be disappointed with your efforts and you will see how I and your celestial helpers will assist in invisible ways – you will be astounded. Each day you put forth time and energy into your heart's work, it will be a day of true productivity.

With much love,
Mary

Daily distractions keep you glued to the TV, movies, video games, or gambling. These are addictive activities that bring no deep satisfaction. Stop all activities that rob you of your life's dreams and energy. Those "entertainments" are just like junk food that only nourish your desires and never your true needs.

Refocus on healthy, life giving activities and shun the imposters that tell you they will bring to you more fun. They lie and only take your money, time, and energy. These are all empty pursuits. You have enough experience now to know that this is the truth.

Instead, go to school, take workshops, learn a new language, exercise, and expand your mind. Go to churches, synagogues, temples, meditation places, and be fed by the spirit. Walk and hike outdoors, bike, seek to find events that feed you as well as entertain.

At some point the critical mass will put down their remotes in unison, disgusted with their choices, and step outside and meet their neighbors, read a book, or learn a new craft. They will be more interested in improving their minds, bodies, and spirits instead of mindless activities that leave them wanting more mindlessness.

Begin right now. Start today by turning off the TV, the video game, or tablet. Turn to the one thing you have in your world that brings you the joy of accomplishment and increases your creativity. Leave the addictive world behind and enter into the new dawn of the good and substantial effort to live richly.

Mary

Mary's Simple Graces

Asking for forgiveness and making amends for wrongs done is a very sacred act. Miracles happen once the slate is clean and there are no more clogs in your cosmic pipes. The flow of Divine energy is free to rush into your life. Prayer, fasting, meditation, are all important as the communication to the Divine is nurtured, but making right the wrongs you've done to others is quiet powerful. You will feel as if you are "walking on air" as you are literally lightening your load.

When a mistake is made, whether intentional or not, a heavy karmic burden attaches to your energy field. It will stay there until that misdeed is mended or atoned. Many just leave it there and come back into another life to make up for something that happened many lifetimes ago. They are unaware what a drain they place on their soul. This is unnecessary if you are aware that you need to clean your record now while you are still in body.

It is especially helpful if you can do this amending in person. This allows the other person the ability to let you know how it affected them, offer consequences, or forgive the debt all together. It is their choice. But if you are open to approaching them, saying that you are sorry and inquiring what you can do to make this right, you have, indeed, done your part.

The angels sing in heaven when this act is performed. You wouldn't believe how what was once a dark, heavy cloud can transform into a shining beam within your energy. This is the way you evolve. It is very enlightening turning a wrong into right, a bad into good. Try it and see what a difference it makes. And as always, do it with me at your side.

Mary

Moving forward into an area that has never been approached before can be a daunting task. Whether it is looking for a job, seeking a new relationship, or beginning the search for a new house, the unknown looks dark when trying to gaze into the future from your present. But do not dismay, the future will become brighter and clearer when you take those first few steps into this process of exploration.

As that first step is taken, more will be revealed. Paths will open, new relationships can form that will help move you from one step to another. Before you know it, you are well into your journey and the goal seems more obtainable and will come slowly into view, even if still far away.

The most important step is the first one. Before you know it you will have that new job, relationship, or home. Looking back, you will see how much you learned, enjoyed, and risked to be where you currently are. As you feel so blessed to be in this better and happier place, you can see how you co-created the outcome by opening yourself to spiritual guidance and your own will to stay on the right path.

All goals are accomplished with that first uncertain and shakey step. So look today at what you can do to finally begin what you have been putting off for so long. This is the day to accomplish one baby step towards a better life.

I am always with you. Call on me to make this a bit more effortless. I love you and I am always ready to assist.

Mary

Open your day with prayer, meditation, and connection to the Divine and me. Praise and be grateful for something in your life even if it is as simple as the bed and sheets. Remember, some do not have either of these. Look out the window to the dawn for a moment as you prepare for the day. Bring in the morning light to illuminate your perspective and brighten your outlook.

As you begin each sunrise with wisdom, connection, and light, you are placing yourself into the flow of universal synchronicity. You will be able to float with the river of life instead of paddling upstream against it. Surprisingly, you will be able to lay back more, enjoy the view, and use the paddles only to steer away from obstacles. Even in the rapids you will be intuitively guiding your boat through rough waters instead of pushing and shoving off the rocks.

The flow will reveal itself to you as you tune in to it early. You can rest assured and appreciate the sun, warmth, air, beauty, and rest – knowing that you have what it takes to negotiate the next challenge as it may come.

Mary

Mary's Simple Graces

When one activity doesn't seem to be working out, shift quickly to something that is. Try not to bulldoze your way into making something happen when it is not. It is frustrating, takes much effort, and usually doesn't work out well anyway. What to do? Put it on hold for awhile and pray for me to help with it. This will give me time to work it out in this dimension and then follow my inspired guidance as I direct you.

Inspiration will come out "of the blue," not on a "To Do" list. All of a sudden you receive an idea to call someone, find another resource, try one more time, or another pathway will be revealed that you didn't know about earlier. You will be amazed that it all works out so easily after you ask for help. That is because I could see the best, easiest, and most profitable direction to take; then, I let you know.

Your frustration and trying too hard are your clues to let go and let God. It's very simple, but hard to let it go and do something else in the moment of exasperation. But look at it from the perspective that it simply is not the right time to resolve this. Sit back and ask what other way you might spend your time now, even have some fun. Let it go. It will be so much healthier to stop and do something else for the time being than to keep trying to do a task or errand that just is not working out.

Give it to me to untangle and to show a different way. Allow time for me to work it out for you. Once you have let it go into my hands, pay light attention to my gentle leading.

With much love,
Mary

So what fun could you have right this minute? What would bring you joy, or at least a sense of accomplishment? What activity would bring the most enjoyment to your heart? Would it be to call a friend, watch a movie, read, or write that book that is waiting for you? Maybe, go have dinner out or watch a game. Run, walk, dance, skip, or just go take a nap. All are important and when you feel just blah and don't want to do anything, do something that will make you feel good – clean the bathtub, make a good meal, go on an errand, or take a hike. Just get out of the space you are in … literally.

When all seems bleak, it is only a matter of changing your perspective, getting a different view, doing something new, taking a risk. Love is all around you and when you look for loving acts to do for yourself and take that first step, decide to get out of your current mindset, it will shift to joy.

Life need not be boring. To get out of a rut – be an adventurer, throw caution to the wind, and step over the cliff into a new lifestyle or environment. Traveling can turn everything around, so go to a different place and meet new people; take an unfamiliar route or talk someone you don't know very well and have a conversation. You never know where a random act of adventure or kindness will lead. It may end you up to a whole new life that starts with one small step forward out of a time of blahs.

Mary

Mary's Simple Graces

I love to give you little surprises: an unexpected day off, a gift of money from an unknown source, or a bit of sunshine on a very rainy day. It thrills my heart when you acknowledge and are grateful for the unexpected. If you complain all the time when you work and when you don't, when it rains and when it doesn't, and when there is too much money or not enough, your life becomes depressing and you will become depressed. But when you look at life and see those surprising little bonuses that are sprinkled throughout your day, it thrills my heart and it will put joy into yours.

I sit with you in these times of astonishment at your good fortune and ponder them as the Divine in your life. See them often, they are there. The friendly sales person, the helpful insurance agent, the loving nurse – are all the work of providence in your life. The more you recognize, are grateful for, and actually well up in appreciation for, the more you will attract such unexpected wonders.

They are graces from a Higher Power. Whether from me, God, or the angels, it matters not, but your heart felt "Thank You" echoes throughout the ethers to our ears and, just as kindly parents, our joy is to give you more of the same. So look for the synchronicity in life and know it is us showering you with blessings. Know we love you so very, very much.

Mary

Draw in money, health, and whatever else you need. Pull it in with your inhale breath. As you breathe in, visualize magnetizing what you want in order to bring it into your sphere. Whether it's a new car, a relationship, or anything your heart desires, take the time to attract it. If your request is not for your highest and best interest, then something even better, the essence of your desire, will be brought to you.

You do not need to be mindful with every breath you take to do this visioning, but if it is done once a day for a few minutes, it will greatly change what is happening in your world. Try it on a global level. Breathe in peace, love, and happiness for all. Sense a pink blanket of comfort for those in need; see green energy floating to those in poverty so they may see the way out. Breathe in kindness and breathe out resolution to those you see in conflict either in close physical vicinity to you or across the world. It does not matter. It will be sent on the wave of your thought and intention, so keep breathing your intercession no matter what you want to use it for.

If your intentions are used for selfish means, to get a better grade without putting in the effort, or winning the lottery, or bringing a love relationship from someone who isn't in love with you, you will only bring an empty vessel. It is best to breathe in the essence of wealth, health, and love. That way the universe will bring it to you in the best way possible for *all* involved. This is not selfish, this is co-creation with spirit.

We love to see when someone surrounds the Earth and her creatures with love, light, and laughter. It brings us together en masse to help put that intention to work. So breathe often, breathe well and, most of all, use it as a means to manifest.

With love and light,
Mary

Joy can be made right where you are, without moving a finger. It is an inner process of shifting thoughts to those of appreciation, love, and healing. If you look constantly at what is wrong, where there is hatred and the fear of disease, you will soon find your energy descending into gloom. But if you continually think about and are grateful for all you have instead of what you do not have; for those you do love and how they love you; thanking those body parts that are working smoothly without you even knowing it – your spirit will soar.

Go forth from this place of joy into your day and see how your thoughts will gravitate to other areas that bring well being to you. You will see these same qualities in others, their health, their love, and their happiness. You won't even notice that others are cranky or negative about the state of the world. Instead, you will be drawn to those who have hope, who illumine the good in the world, and see through the eyes of love. These are the ones to surround yourself with. They will bring their happiness to add to your own.

It is a wonderful time to be alive and all is in Divine order,
Mary

Sometimes I just have to stop you so I can get your attention and talk to you. The world and your mundane activities of errands, responsibilities, sleeping, eating, socializing, friends, and family can take up all your time so that I fall to the bottom of the priority list. So when you find yourself without your phone, computer, people, and all alone in a deserted place, it is time to go within and find me.

The alternative is to put me on TOP of your To Do List, to connect with me early, even before you get out of bed. Call on me, say your rosary, and ask me to be with you in all you do that day. Then and only then, will your life be placed on a much higher plane. The other items on your list will go so much smoother or something much more important will happen that day because I am working with you.

I am here for you, but you must ask in order for me to activate such power for you. If you postpone your time with me until all is done, you do a disservice to yourself and others. A lovely energy, a healing salve, a brighter outcome would be yours. Ask for the best in all – ask for me.

Loving you,
Mary

Commerce is at its best. You are able to buy or acquire everything you need to live a very wealthy life. Many of you live in a city that offers whatever you need within a few blocks or miles. Others live a rural life where they may have to buy more on the internet and have it shipped. It has never, ever been easier to get whatever you need.

Not so long ago, people would travel great distances to get their supplies. Even before that, medicine, goods, and services were not available. People were forced to do without and had a shortened life span due to this. But now, everything that is needed is available. The only thing that is not bought instantly with a credit card or money, is your connection to spirit.

Some have thought that if they go to a weekend spiritual retreat with a person who has found enlightenment, they too could breathe in this same glow. They are so disappointed that their anxiety, depression, and worries return within a short time. They learned certain tricks and techniques to connect with spirit but failed to have the discipline to actually follow through once the world's clamor nudged in and drowned out that small inner voice.

Again, ask for me early, join me in spirit early each and every day. See how this simple conversation and sitting in my presence can lift your soul and spirits. I am there for you always. All you need to do is stop and ask.

Mary

All is in Divine order, even when it doesn't seem as if there is any Divine presence in a given situation. Source is very close in times of crisis or need. Pay attention to even the most minuet synchronicity.

First pray and then step forward with any inspired action. Simply begin and be open to being gently led to the next step. Notice the Divine in it all. Appreciate what happens. Who came into your life at just the right time, what information and insight came out of the wide blue yonder? This is God and I guiding you to the next right action and person.

Stay in gratitude instead of fear and anger when the unexpected occurs. It is all for your highest and best! You will see this when all is said and done. You will be amazed how one right action leads to another and where you are at the end is such an improved life.

Just as your car flashes "check engine" and something begins to make noise that wasn't present before, this is the time to pray … immediately! Get your celestial mechanics on the job. They are there instantly to diagnose and resolve the problem. Emotionally step back and watch the miracles happen. All is in Divine order.

Mary

I am always here, even in your sleep, God and I are working for you. We never sleep. Give us your problems at night and let us work on them as you have a good, deep rest. Then in the morning, be open to new thoughts and visions while you pray and thank the Divine for another day.

Give us your day to guide as you step into your morning. Remember us often throughout the day, say thank you and listen to our subtle urgings. We will always be there for you.

When you see or hear something that is not in harmony, something unloving, pray for me to be with that person, situation, or event. Say the rosary or simply ask for my grace to surround the circumstances. Know and trust that I will do what is best for all involved. There is no disaster that I cannot help. Simply release it into my hands and heart. I will be there in less than a second to shift the energy to a higher plane.

There is nothing, nothing, at all that God or I can not do. Just trust me with all, even the impossible. I have access to and can ask for intercession from angels, Jesus, and the Divine. Just trust, let it go and see what happens. Praise me, praise God, and raise the vibrations to the highest level humanly possible. All is well … All is well … All is well.

With much love,
Mary

Be in nature – go to the mountains, the ocean, the desert. See what wonders there are in creation. Go to national parks, to places that are marked as scenic, get off road, surround yourself in the woods, the fields, and the waters of the Earth. This cleansing of your spirit is vital for your good health and healing.

Nourish yourself with dirt, plants, and moisture. Bring in the life force of all there is in the world. Bring it in with your sight, touch, and smell. See the beauty around you. Sit and immerse yourself into the environment. Be still and allow the spirit of nature to fill you to the top – overflowing.

Pray and meditate within this beauty. Bless and release all that you want to renew while you are sitting on the Earth. Stand and breathe in all that is available within this pristine world. Smell the wildflowers, the rain, the snow, the mountain. Know it intimately. Be in one place long enough so that you know when it is time to return as a lover knows it is time to call the beloved who is not present. You will sense a longing and feel nature's call for your soul to come, refresh, and reconnect.

We are always with you. Know that deeply – please never doubt,
Mary

Sweeping the floor of your mind will till your thoughts to give fertile ground for new ideas to land and grow like seeds. So if something from the past is invading your thinking or you have fears of the future, visualize yourself weeding the walls and floors of your mind. Send the debris out the door. Let the wind blow through your mind and negative thinking will disappear into the ethers.

Then spray, brighten, and sprinkle with the sunshine of life. Lay down a carpet of thick positive affirmative nutrients. Allow those seedlings to have the light, moisture, and fertilizer to grow and flourish. Watch your garden populate with good, strong, and sturdy crops of creative notions, insights, and inventions. The new will replace the dry, worn out, and broken thinking that has been scattered about in your inner world.

Harvest what you have tended, bringing in the overflowing baskets of creative ideas. These will feed the world with your new creations and the healthy power of your thoughts.

Mary

More and more you are losing your ability to speak your truth using your oral capacity. Communication technology is important for the advancing culture, but when it breaks down, the default is to use the old techniques that are built into your bodies. The apparatus is on your face – it is to open your mouths and speak.

Do you see that social skills are declining? The art of conversation is shifting to electronic tablets, texting, Twitter, and Facebook. Once the electricity is pulled, these are all useless. So be aware not to let your oral communications lapse into disuse. Use and improve your speaking, reasoning, and communication skills. In the future, you will see that these all are extremely important.

The Earth is changing and when there are catastrophic changes and the use of technology is limited, if existing at all, the only way to get the word out is verbally and intuitively.

You will be greatly handicapped if all your needs are limited to appliances, cars, and heat that are dependent on a human-made power source too.

Continue to invent and financially support solar, wind, water, and alternative sources of energy to continue your current quality of life. If you put all your needs into the current electrical dependency, when that is no longer available, your quality of life and, indeed, your life itself, will be in jeopardy. It is ok to use this source that is so available now, but it is wise to put part of your household, business, and transportation needs into alternative power sources. That way, no matter what goes on outside your windows and doors, you and your family will be sustained throughout the duration.

Think ahead by looking at past natural disasters and what would have been helpful to those victims as they were paralyzed by the storm or disaster. Would an energy source powered by the sun, wind, or water have been sustaining? Indeed it would have. So while there is yet time, look closely at where you can diversify your energy needs and begin to shift some of them over to sustainable sources.

Mary

Talk to me often. I love to hear what you are doing, how you are feeling, and if there is anyway for me to be of assistance. Meditation is listening to my voice, my inner urging, and insights. Be with me in silence, either lying down, sitting, or standing facing the sun, breeze, or ocean. It does not matter where you are; just seek my presence – everywhere.

Being away from the distractions of the world would be best, of course, but you need only to ask and I will come immediately – wherever you are.

Seek me upon awakening and then again throughout your day and before you retire at night. Surround your day with my connection and knowledge. All is grand when placed on this higher plane. You know so well how to reach me. It is so simple … just call my name.

"Mary, please come be with me."

"Mary, please help me."

"Mary, please fill me with your grace."

Whatever you ask for shall be given. It will be in a form that will be of the highest good benefit for all concerned. So seek me often and with great expectation. I will not disappoint. I am always available to you.

Lovingly,
Mary

Dishonesty breaks a connection. If you tell someone an untruth, the connection between you is frayed. If it continues or more lies are told, then the cords of trust and relationship are weakened until there is finally a break. The severing can occur suddenly when the dishonesty is discovered. All the cords retreat quickly as from an imminent danger. This is similar to a retreat from a hot flame or surface.

These old cords will never be repaired from such singeing. New cords of attachment will cautiously be explored to see if you are trustworthy again, after an apology or forgiveness, but it will be tentative at best. A long road of amend making, reparations, and trust building could enable an attachment to reoccur, but this is very hard to do for the person who broke the trust in the first place.

The victim of this deceit will need time to be in shock, to grieve, or even lash out for the damage done to their energy, love, and good faith. Prayer and energy healing take time and effort. Just as the body takes time to heal itself, so does the emotional body require a period of quiet retreat to return to health.

Of course, the best course of action is to be honest in all your dealings so no trust will ever be severed and whole relations between people will grow and thrive. But on this planet, you are here to experiment with duality – the positive and negative.

Growing can occur as the result of a series of your own mistakes, or it can be learned from another's failings so you will not have to experience this yourself. So stay open to the wisdom of other's shortcomings. Instead of judging their actions and consequences, breathe in what they have learned, question them so it is very clear what their experiences and feelings are and how the negative action affected all involved. This way you too will grow without the pain or the penalties. Bless them for doing it for you. They have actually done you a great favor.

Mary

Mary's Simple Graces

Good friends are hard to come by, so keep up with communication and connection with each and every one. What is a "good friend?" It is someone who you can rely on for the truth, for support, and who will be there in a crisis.

Some have friends who are available for only the fun times. Those are enjoyable, but not what you call good friends. Some are companions for the movies or who can share common interests. Those too are important, but not what I am talking about. The ones I am talking about are the "salt of the Earth." They are there for you when the chips are down, when you are not able to party or when you need someone to really talk to without worry of gossip or criticism. They love you in a deep part of themselves and show this love when you need it the most.

So have lots of buddies or friendships, but the relationships that need to be nurtured the most are the steadfast, proven-by-fire friends who stick with you through thick and thin. They are the most important treasures on this Earth. They will be there for you no matter what. Honor them, thank them, and support them as well. You will be doubly blessed to know such a one and to actually have them in your inner circle.

Mary

You are so weary of worry. When you lay your head on the pillow, your mind thinks it now has your complete attention and will talk to you about all the horrible things that could happen or did happen. No matter how much you tell it to go to sleep and be quiet, it takes the opportunity to say, "And another thing ..." On and on it goes.

"Is there no stopping?" You ask me. "Is there no relief from this constant fret?" "Won't you just knock me out so I can have a sweet slumber and be refreshed in the morning where all will look so much brighter?" It is your job to focus your mind, to co-create a peaceful world in and out. Yes, you have to harness these wild horses of thought and corral them into peacefulness but I can guide you with how to do that. But you have to take the action.

One way to calm these turbulent waves of inner chatter is to meditate more. Listening is the key. Stay between the words of your mind, the blank spaces. Also, please limit energizing supplements after a certain time of day. Everyone is unique, it is up to you to notice your own cut off point for coffee, tea, power drinks, or vitamins. Allow drowsiness and accept that evening time is a time to relax.

Be aware of what you do later in the day, what you watch on TV, read in books, conversations, and especially put on hold any important decisions or discussions with yourself or others regarding large or pending issues. As a business closes its doors at a certain time, you also need to limit your mind's business hours. Visualize a "Closed" sign on the door of your mind and feel the appreciation of a job well done for that day. In the morning after you have completed your self care, watch yourself turn that sign over, so it reads: "Open, Come On In!" Your thoughts can be trained.

I am always open for business, so ask me to continue guiding your mental, spiritual, and physical well-being as you drift into your nightly dreams and slumber. I love you!

Goodnight,
Mary

Good Orderly Direction = GOD. It is doing those activities that bring you a feeling of accomplishment, joy, gratitude, and fulfillment. You feel it instantly. It feels good on the deep level of the soul.

When you are engaged in addictive, non-productive, or harmful activities, the life force you value so much is actually drained from your body. These activities need your life force to continue way beyond normal and, afterward, you feel depleted, unfulfilled, and drained. But how do you turn from these exciting but harsh enterprises and put your time and energy into those actions that will improve, fulfill, and express creativity? How do you resist an energetic habit that pulls you into its shadowy arms? Once in its tight grip, there seems no way to get free until it throws you to the ground, battered, and you fall into a fitful sleep of shame and guilt for succumbing again to the temptation of that same old behavior.

There is a way out. It is to not engage in such activities in the first place. It sounds so simple, but difficult to do. The trick is not to begin. Where are the people who are creative, improving, and spending their time and energy on activities that fulfill and give joy? You will find them in the classrooms, studios, and spiritual centers. They may be tired after a day of work/play but they feel a strong sense of accomplishment. They rest in peace and invention is in their dreams.

Guard your time and energy well. Dole it out in the best possible ways that are adding to your life instead of depleting it. If you never initiate an addictive process at the beginning, you will never get hooked again. Be mindful of that initial step and the thought, "I am going to do this for only this amount of time." Know that it is impossible to break once you go down that road. The addictive process does take over and will not allow you to stop until *it* is finally exhausted, not when *you* desire.

We are always there for you no matter what choices you make, but the regret of a life wasted is sad and lonely. So turn now to Good Orderly Direction. See what is in front of you that requires your attention and do that. As you take those first few steps, then the next steps will be revealed. By the end of the day, you will fall into bed with a smile for all that you have accomplished and end with a prayer of thanksgiving for a day well spent.

Mary

Mary's Simple Graces

Denial is often used to ignore something that is not part of the world view as one sees it. Instead of changing a set-in-stone perspective of reality in the world, some will just deny its existence. They just will not look at it, ask about it, or give it any attention. They will simply say that either it is not so or rationalize the truth to fit their limited belief system.

Eventually, though, there comes a point that those who deny will finally be forced to face the uncomfortable, either in a forceful way, or in a moment of inspiration that awakens the sleeping consciousness which in turn will cause a paradigm shift.

It can be a very hard battle to show someone the blatant facts of what they are ignoring. Many wars, debates, and protests occur just to shift this ignorance. Ignoring a new reality can be quite shattering. Either way, change and expansion of consciousness is the way of the world.

This Universe is expanding. It is best to be flexible and open to all experiences and beliefs. That way denial will be limited to only the closed-minded and the doors will be opened to the ones who value others and new experiences. Much pain and suffering can come from such denial, but love will finally open the door.

Some even say that I do not exist, that my spirit and love died with my body. No matter how much I appear to people in the world, some people will call visionaries names like "crazy" or "evil" while others will just say you have simply been led astray and they will pray for you.

There are those, though, who will appreciate the service you provide to those seeking answers and the touch of higher dimensions. These are the ones you need to call in. Be visible and verbal so they can find you, even though it leaves the door open to scoffers. It will let in many believers who need to know the truth. Your work is valuable. Go in faith and with my blessing.

Mary

Assisting others is helpful, but it doesn't mean for you to live their lives for them. It may mean you nudge someone in the right direction. Open the door, show them the way. Then, if they hesitate, you can encourage, love, and even push them into the wide blue yonder of the future. You know they will land safely, but they are too fearful to take that last step on their own. They may need the well placed kick out the door.

You can remember being dragged lovingly into your future time, so you can be expert in doing that for someone else. They have a parachute, they have an emergency kit, they have all they need except the one bit of courage to jump. This is your role – to assist others.

So move forward into this service and remember this the next time you yourself have to take a leap of faith. Just do it and dive into trust. We will help you fly through the thin air and put your attention on the view and adventure of the flight instead of the fear of an unknown future.

We love you and are always your life preserver. You will do well, and at the end of the trip, you will want to do it all over again … and again … and again.

Mary

Mary's Simple Graces

When you need help, it is easier than you think. Your mind will tell you that there is no one who can help you; you have to do it all by yourself. That is not true. It is quite simple. Ask. Just as I have mentioned many times, you can connect with me simply by asking. To receive the help you need on the physical plane, the same is true. Ask. But then you say, "Who do I ask?" Ask the Universe, the sky, God. The right help will come at the right time when you ask.

There are always celestial helpers who can respond to your request. Your action is to pray, affirm, open to receive, and allow assistance to enter. This will magnetize the aid needed. But most of all, ask me for help and I will guide you to the best way to find what you are looking for. Let me know all the details and be open to receive whatever comes along.

Anything from me will be in your best interest and all involved, even though it may not seem so at the time. But as you look back you will agree that it was the best option possible. I am always there to support you and there is always an abundance of assistance abound. Simply ask; we will ALL help.

Mary

You have heard, "Do what you can and God will do the rest" or "Do what you can and leave the outcome to God." This is only partially true. It is important to follow Divine guidance *before* you do anything of major importance. Of course, if you are in a burning building, get out and talk to God later. But for those decisions that are long term or allow time for prayer, discernment, and meditation before an action has to be made, wait for your intuition to lead you to the right path.

You have free will. So, when you ask for a Divine consult, know that you are seeking a higher perspective and take what you intuit into account. If you are seeking only God's will, then it is easier to follow because there will be little conscious debate about which road to take. The highest path will open up to you and you will be assured that it is a better way by the amount of synchronicity, coincidental signs, and by the ease of your travels toward it. Almost like a flow down a river. One step will lead to the next without much effort.

Having said that though, there are rocky trails to traverse in this lifetime as well. Those will provide you with much character building. They are so "right" and they lead to truth, justice, and love so that you will not mistake them for the wrong way. These paths sometimes are difficult and require courage, but the reward of doing the "right" and "good" thing will outweigh the burden of the trip.

No matter your course, I am always with you. Never are you left alone to slug it out just to fail. At any time, just ask and I will send resources ... always.

With much love,
Mary

When the weather turns cold, you may desire to stay in, cozy up with a good book, a warm bath, and spend the evening with your essence. I will put a sweet, pink blanket of energy around you as the snow and rain falls. Stay in the security of spirit by meditating and bringing us in to be with you tonight and forever.

The rosary is a powerful way to begin our time together, whether it is a night in, or a day out. Focus on the words, stay with me as long as you are able, for I am here for you. Surround yourself with my cloak of peace and joy. All will look better when I am in your conscious presence.

You can push the reset button any time during your day or night – reset with me. Begin again and ask for me to take root in your soul. I grow there in the most exotic ways.

As roses bud and blossom, so will your spirit flower with delight to have the sunshine of unconditional, sacred love blessing you. I love you with more than my heart – my very being loves you dearly.

Mary

Spark the flame of hope, dreams, and future wishes. Fan those burning embers into a torch of action and bring your light into the world for the improvement of all. Those embers within need your breath and attention, then watch them become a roaring fire again with the right fuel and focused intent. You too can ignite your flames into a bonfire of love into right, wonderful action.

So if you think that your light has either burnt out or just diminished with neglect, think again, oh dear one. It is only languishing in the depths of your being – waiting for your attention, which will throw on some timber and blow the winds of spirit that way again.

Remember I am of the light, unconditional love, holy fire, and part of the Divine kindle for your individual blaze. Stir until sparks catch from the glowing orange embers. Your fire has not gone out, it is only dormant for a bit. At any time you may rekindle it into the wildfire of Divine love.

Mary

The faithful will inherit the Earth. It means to keep the faith when it looks as if there is no hope for change or something better to come. The future is hidden from view so you must focus on this day only and what you can do. Yes, it is important to make plans, but allow spirit time to work for you too.

Pray and ask for our help. Then, do what you can each day, and let it go. Let the worry go. Let the rehearsal of the future go and shift your thoughts to what is in front of you. It may be to take a shower, or to show up at the job, or just to call a friend in need. Do whatever you can to take your attention off the problem and let it be in our hands. Turn to what is in your power to change – the oil in the car, go grocery shopping, or finish a project.

We are so there for you, but sometimes your worrying impedes our progress. We are only energy and when your willful thoughts come blasting through or you pray, over and over again, desperately for help, we have to stop our work to comfort you. If you would see to it that you take care of your thoughts and not let them throw you into panic, if you practice faith, praise, and let it go, we will all be much better off and your answers will come quicker than you think. Try it if you don't believe me.

The next time you have a conflict or problem, exercise your faith muscles. Make those as strong as you can. You won't even have to be sore in the morning from over use as you would with a physical muscle. It will only bring you greater joy as you utilize your faith.

We are ALWAYS there for you. Believe it when you need it the most. After the miracle comes, then you know for sure we were there, but know it even in times of turmoil. We are there working for your highest and best.

Loving you,
Mary

Stress is the sign of working too hard, not enough self care and too much going on in your head. At times, it just can't be helped. If you repeatedly take on too much, can't say no to a request, or just have overstepped your energy level, then ask for help. We can help you learn the lesson of what you truly can handle with grace and joy. Because most of the time, you have the power to limit the amount on your plate.

You are in human form and can not take on as much as you could when you were in spirit. I can take on the world. There is no time and space where I reside so each request can be answered in Divine timing. You do not have that privilege. You have to work within physical limitations.

Work within your own limits too. Be aware of what you can and cannot do to achieve the best results. Then, rest well knowing you have done all that you are able to do with the energy and time that you have that day.

What other avenues can be taken to assist you in all you want to accomplish? If you do not know your own boundaries, your body will begin to rebel and illness or injury will result. It is time to let it all go and initiate another softer, more serene way to fulfill your dreams.

Mary

Shopping is such a joy, seeing all the beautiful colors, fabrics, jewels, metals, but I especially love the scarves. My passion was scarves, shawls, and robes. We had very little to choose from, but the fabrics were the finest. The colors were a bit subdued in contrast with what is offered now. It is very fun to go shopping with you and see what is available.

Dress in your finest, always, when you go out the door. It is important to offer beauty to others and it will increase your confidence and outlook on your daily life. Wear whatever makes you happy and guards against the weather.

My "veil", as they call it, was of the finest cloth and I used it for many occasions. It was a gift from Joseph and I cherished it. It seemed to be a protection for me too, being surrounded with my husband's love and honor. He didn't live long after we were married, but I loved him so. I never married again, but devoted my life to my son's work and to his followers. They were so good to me.

So enjoy shopping, take me along if you wish, I am with you always.

Loving you,
Mary

Hope is eternal. Find and share it everyday. There are always people who need that smile, that touch, and the message of hope. Find them and tell them that all will change in a moments notice if they but wait and shift their inner life and turn to the One who loves them most – the most highest God. At the point of shifting the focus to "On High," to the light of the Divine, angels will flock to embrace and set into motion trains of circumstances you call miracles.

Sometimes a person is so deep in the well of despair that the angels need to slowly lift them out knowing that to catapult them into the light would put them into panic. So, lovingly, they slowly turn up the light. Angels elevate them higher and higher, ever so slowly as they get used to each step of the way. So try to be patient with us. We know what we are doing. Search and rescue is our game. We are pros in this activity.

Now about you, remember to always keep your face toward God, pray in the morning for God's will to be done and ask for Divine presence each day. Ask angels to surround you with Divine light and they will choose the color of the day that will assist you most. Each day is a new dawn, a new life, and new possibilities are available that just weren't there yesterday. Rejoice in the morning light and fill your heart with joy as if dipping into a shimmering pool of light. You are never alone ... just ask.

Mary

Yes, it is time to move forward with completing all tasks. Take the time, put the effort into your ideas, and see them flourish. Do whatever you can to see that it happens. We are so there for you, but you see there is just so much we can do. We cannot do it for you. You have free will. We can only help from here by giving insight, circumstances, and synchronicity. You have to step forward and take the action.

We are very excited about new ideas. They are good ones. You have studied about what works well, so just move forward. The slow way isn't always the best way. There are amazing technologies for you to learn about and utilize. Take some classes and be educated in the areas needed. Just let it be known that you are working and projects will be completed at a quick rate. You can do it all, work, have a life, and play as much as you want. You just have to focus your efforts into what will give you the most for your time. We are there for you. Now get going.

Mary

Pain in the body is usually associated with an imbalance of the energy system before it manifests into a physical ailment. For instance, headaches could also be a sign of too much pressure in a person's life, or too much worry about situations that need some action, or, at the very least, prayer and letting go. Of course, the first line of defense is to see a health care practitioner to work on the symptoms and causes, but it is also important to work on the energy imbalance – the root of all dis-ease.

Your soul or aura has many layers and they are deeply effected by what you think and do. If there is an over abundance of a difficult or negative emotion, the energy system tries to balance it. It is the way of nature, to seek balance in all.

When it is a chronic problem or an abundance of negativity, the system will get out of whack. When this occurs, a dis-ease or un-easiness is felt by you and it will continue until either the energy is stabilized and healed or it will get worse until you realize that you need to shift your way of being. We are always available to help in these cases.

You have many on earth who have written extensively about these manifested health problems that are an emotional, mental, or spiritual imbalance. They also have very helpful suggestions and affirmations that will provide relief and actually improve the health of your body, if you use what they have to offer.

So give thanks for that part of your body that is telling you there is an imbalance because it is warning you of major problems to come if it is not addressed now. What a wonderful vehicle our souls have chosen to encase themselves in. It is very clever how the body pushes the panic button and then slowly heals itself when the message has been taken seriously.

Mary

Jealousy is an emotion of fear. Fear of losing what you think you have or want. It can easily be remedied by understanding, allowing another to make their own choices, and by finding the root cause of said jealousy.

It is important not to act out in a jealous rage and to step back, pause, regroup, and find the core of the emotion. If someone's actions continue to bring up jealousy, it is important to work on yourself first and then discuss a possible solution with the other person. If there is no solution that is agreeable, then it may be time to part ways and take time to go within on a deeper level and search out the causes of such strong reactions. If this work is not done, you may attract an even more deceitful lover or friend until you do the inner work that needs to be done to heal this old wound in you.

Jealousy is a touchstone of a troubled and hurt time in a person's past that will need much love and support. Comfort and teach that damaged part to react in an alternative way when these feelings arise. Much healing can occur from jealousy.

You are never alone and will always be taken care of by your celestial support: by me, by the Divine, and by the angels. It isn't always easy to accept when all you are focused on is a physical love or support. But in time you will realize that we are the most important love and support you will ever need. When I say that, I do mean ever need – as in eternity.

Love yourself, don't abandon yourself and be kind to that injured part that went through so much trauma. Know that you, yourself will never leave you. Take yourself into your own loving arms and tell yourself that you are the lover, the friend, and the parent you long for – true and loyal. Then, so much less will be demanded from those around you. We love you and never leave!

Mary

It is so human to put off these important spiritual contacts in order to do the physical plane activities. Much can distract from a soul connection. That is why you are all here – to learn to focus primarily on the spiritual realm and allow it to rise up during your day, as cream rises on fresh milk. Give the spiritual experience the best you have to offer, at your freshest. Do not make it the last thing you do at night, exhausted from your day.

We are always patient for we know how difficult it is to give us a priority. To put primary your spiritual health and well-being. Once that is accomplished, then, you can go about your business with a song in your heart, lightness of being, and the ability to sail through all your other activities with greater heart, intuition, and synchronicity.

You can try again tomorrow. Put me first, do what I say in your morning meditation and it will carry you through the rest of your day.

Always,
Mary

Today is about letting go of what people think of you. Better yet, to let go of what *you* think people think of you and turn your thoughts to me and to the joy in your life. Sometimes the very thought of people and how they will criticize you will make you stop taking beneficial action. Look at your movies and books. Many stories are about how someone had the courage to do what was right with social, friends, and family pressures to do otherwise. That is what I want for you to learn. Step forward into a life of right action for *you*.

There will always, I repeat, ALWAYS be those critics who do not want change. Then there are those who are jealous or afraid themselves. All these people will throw invisible cords of their own will around you. They want you to conform to their negative and judgmental way of believing and thinking. Do not let that happen. Cut those cords with the mighty sword of the angels. Break free of what you have heard is right or wrong. If it is the spiritual and most heartfelt choice for you, then it is right for everyone.

You do not owe anyone allegiance except your God. So stay close to Divine will and know that there will always be opposition to the better, more humane way. You are supported by higher celestial forces, me included, to do the best action for yourself. We all love and surround you at this time of brave decisions.

Mary

Breathe in the air and sunshine of a new day. Let the rain fall upon your head and body, cleansing your energy field. Sometimes one will shower or bathe a physical body, but then protect themselves from the very natural forces that are available to freshen the energy surrounding you.

Prayer and meditation will also cleanse your spirit. Walking into a personal sanctuary, leaving any burdens at my feet and at the feet of the Divine will set your heart free. Leave all those cares and worries. Face the day with a new perspective of hope, joy, and faith.

I am always with you – even in your darkest hour. I am always with you in your peak of joy. I just am always with you. Period.

Come to me often and see what I hold in my hands for you. Receive all I have, all my daily graces to help with your everyday walk. Sit by me, look at me, sing with me. You will hear the bird's song, the humming of the bees, and the rush of the waters more clearly as you commune with me. All I ask, is that you come.

Mary

Enemies can be as the chatter of squirrels in a tree. But if you have a rattlesnake close at hand, beware of their fatal bite. When enemies are rattlesnakes, the best way to handle them is with prayer, courage, a quick retreat, or removal of the danger. But it is an operation that needs great skill, experience, and bravery to accomplish. So, when you plan your counter-attack, find out how dangerous your enemy truly is, then plan accordingly.

As a family, we had many, many enemies. When someone challenges the authorities, the established organizations, and the social mores, people can get very frightened and lash out. So when confronting a foe, great strategy is important. I can help guide you in times for opposing evil.

Sometimes it is better to flee, sometimes it is time to confront, and other times it is necessary to die for your values. You choose the best way to deal with the enemy. God is always with you as each situation unfolds.

Look to yourself and what you are learning also and try not to repeat it. Usually, one can tell at first sight if someone will be a friend or foe. True nature comes out later. Once known, it is best to leave as quickly and with as much grace as possible. Those people have no conscience about what they say or do. You are no match for the unscrupulous.

Remember, I will help you in whatever way you decide. All is truly well even though it doesn't seem like it. You will come out unscathed, just stay on track with what you want to do.

All is well,
Mary

See where crisis offers great opportunity and use it for your advantage. It may be God clearing the way as an answer of your prayers.

When surprises happen, it can be fun to see how the universe works in wondrous ways. It can also bring up anger and fear for those who do not like change. So, when shocking news comes your way, step back and allow the shock to wash over you. Let it settle in and then allow yourself to be on different footing. All of a sudden, much has changed around you, but you remain the same.

If it isn't an emergency, allow the change to occur and let yourself find solid ground. Take as long as you need to make wise decisions. When one reacts hastily in these situations, one is often wrong. Take your time in your decision process, but also see the opportunities that cracking the mundane egg can bring and try not to be too immobilized so you can take advantage of the opportunities as they presents themselves.

Sometimes, though, you will find that if it is a work situation, some people will shift out of the job just because it is too much change. If you stay, allowing others to leave, an opportunity for a higher, better position may open up. Then, it will be time for you to step forward and receive what earlier was not available to you.

Loving you,
Mary

Loving what is brings gratitude to your heart. If you are in a hard place, nothing seems to be going your way, and you are hanging on by a boot strap, start singing songs of praise and gratitude. Sing those tunes that have joy in them and are so happy that they make you want to sing at the top of you lungs. Blast it out!

As you belt those lyrics out, the vibration of even the worst situation cannot help but improve. You will change the energy around it and something is sure to tumble. Sing those songs in private, in a group, or wherever you can to lift your spirit and emotions. Fear cannot stand the music of praise. So turn up the volume, open the windows, and sing, sing, sing!

We will all join you in your hymns of love and awe. While we are all gathered, enjoying your worship, pray intensely, just as if you are at a wonderful family reunion and after a great meal you ask all your relatives for help. We will not let you down, but will shower you with tremendous love and support through difficult waters.

Mary

The storms of life are navigable. But you need a very good navigator. I can be that for you. Just ask and I will guide you through even the most treacherous waters, mountains, and valleys. In order to go on such a dangerous journey there has to be trust in your captain. Trust me in everything. Bring the worst problem or request to me and it will be answered in the best possible way.

Give me time to work it out, to put the pieces into place for you so there will be an even better solution than you could have possibly come up with, even with expert human aid. Now I am not saying that I don't use those around you to help. I am saying that they are all at a disadvantage when I am not brought into the equation. With me guiding you through the dark side of the soul, you can have clear vision throughout the journey.

Trust me, remember me, and you will go far and safely. I am always a beacon of light.

Mary

Let's go shopping! It is so clearing and it brightens everyone's energy especially when we find treasures that feel great to you. If you are a conscious shopper, only spending within your budget and thoughtfully analyzing the item carefully to ask yourself if you absolutely love it and will use it, then good for you, for you have a house of treasures.

Always pick your color and fit. Make sure everything is perfect, not almost perfect or it will do. You know you will never wear or use it if that is the case. The joy you have in your loved and cherished items will foster love and beauty for you and those around you.

The money always comes, just as it does when you want to put gas in the car or food on the table. Money manifests easily for you when you need it. Trust this more and more. Even though you would like to have extra in your bank account, you can create it in another dimension, in your imagination and draw it to you into the physical plane. See it, feel it, know it is yours – then enjoy it by spreading it throughout and into the world. Allow others to feel the abundance around you.

Just stay open to my gentle guidance today. I love to go on lighter missions. Let's go shop for those things that bring you such joy and nourishment.

Lovingly,
Mary

Yes, be still and sit awhile with me. Allow the silence and contemplation of all you see fill you from this quiet place. Just look around, not to "see" anything, just lightly aware of your life with me. Talk to me if you must, but mostly listen.

Learn and feel what are the sensations of your body. Feel the breeze, the temperature of the warm earth beneath your feet, smell the dryness of the air, the sound of a far away bird, the rustling of leaves, people shuffling by. See the sunset, the colors changing the clouds in the sky, the mountains throwing shadows. All of it, bring it in to me.

Silently, quietly, sense your world, Divine creation – all for you. So many are in the world but do not take the time to sit and enjoy what is so freely given to them. Be one that notices, is grateful for, and can see in depth the slow rhythm of nature.

What would that tree be doing at midnight, at noon, in the summer, winter, and fall. Would the birds tickle the branches with their light feet or the leaves with their wings? Quietly … slowly … nature lives. Be as one with nature intentionally, see what is in your vicinity, in your neighborhood, in your backyard, and wherever you are with me. Let me open your inner and outer senses to what is really going on around you. Turn off the TV, quit the errands, come, come, and sit awhile with me.

Tenderly,
Mary

To make money, you will have to open more avenues for money to flow into your bank accounts and hands. So think not so much how to save and budget, even though that is important, but how to create added income producing strategies. You only have so much time to put into working. It is about working smarter, not harder. Please rid yourself of the belief that in order to receive twice your income, you have to work twice as hard or twice the hours. That is not the case, it is about believing that there are creative ways to have your time and money work for you while you maintain the same level of energy.

For example, if you have a product, you can sell it to retail or on-line outlets who will sell it for you instead of you selling one at a time. You will sell multiple units. You have only to convince the one who will buy many items and peddle them for you. That way you are not at every store personally selling. Likewise, if you purchase a business that is already successful, you do not have to create it from scratch. You can then use your expertise and make it even more successful.

We are in this together. Co-create with me creative ways that are successful. Now stay with me as I teach you about ways to bring in abundance. Be silent for a while to hear my voice.

Mary

Congratulations are in order when you come up to milestones of achievement. Yes, we do help, but we could not do it without your action, your effort, your asking, and allowing our assistance. We are always there for you whenever you call. Let us step in when you come to obstacles and we will blast them out of the way.

We are more anonymous when life is going well, smoothly. But you notice our intervention when you have done all you can and we just gently move the challenge to one of learning instead of being an unmovable roadblock. You see what we can do so you think we have done it all, but that is not true. You, my dear ones, are the brave ones stepping forward in your work and making a change. We follow your leads.

Remember to call on us more and more each and every day. We will be there with banners, pompoms, and big bands to cheer you on and to tackle the opposing forces so you have a clear and straight path to the goal line. Work hard, but work with us.

Mary

Mary's Simple Graces

Love everyone! Does not mean that you must like them, but love them for being human, for taking the chance to come to this world and for living a life with all its struggles. You never know what people have to deal with in life or why they are the way they are, but you can help them by sending them the vibration of love.

If you are on a plane, a bus, a train, a subway, or in a store, send love to all who are with you. Blanket the whole lot of them with sweet pink. Send a feeling of love before you enter into a challenging situation. Ask for the energy of love to precede you, to guide you to the next loving sentence or act. Be true to who you are … and choose love.

Love changes everything for the better. It may not seem like it at first, but it is true. When love is liberally applied, all will find their right path, the true way and follow their own beam of love. If there is negative energy, it can not tolerate so much love around and will leave to find its own level.

I send you love all the time – Divine, unconditional love, the very best there is. You can only grow and be enhanced by the flow of such goodness.

Loving you,
Mary

When there is a long absence from contact with spirit, do not think we leave you. We are with you in other ways. If your life has a crisis or transition that pulls you away from meditation, prayer, or your spiritual practice, know that the connection is not lost.

We don't want everyone to stop their lives and live a "Holy Life" away from the tasks at hand. No, we want to co-create with you so that your spiritual journey manifests in actions and work that is of service to the world. That is a holy life.

That may translate into building a family, attending to the plumbing problem, or being with friends. As you know, the path of spirit is not a life away from the duties of this world, it is being fully involved – being *with* me in the world. Call the Divine and me into everything you do – from the mundane to the deepest depths of spiritual growth. We are a spiritual family. Even though you are not with your physical, extended family all the time, they are a part of you and your daily living. Same with us; we are with you each step of the way.

So you are never alone – making decisions, putting out fires, changing lanes in the car. We are always with you clearing the path, softening a heart, or exposing a truth that has to be dealt with. Look for evidence of us, our footprints in life. Watch for the coincidences and synchronicity and you will find our handywork.

We love you always.
Mary

When you feel tired, it may be me asking you to sit, be still, and talk to me awhile – to renew your spirit, body, and mind with my refreshing presence. Some will immediately seek caffeine in a soda, tea, or coffee. But for those who do not wish to override their natural rhythms, time with spirit, stillness, and silence will bring insight, energy, and deep connection with the strength of the universe.

It is up to you to choose. Do you want an artificial stimulant that is temporary or do you want me? Which is more organic, freeing, and non-addictive? When you want mindlessness, you can turn on the TV, videos, and games, or go into a meditative state and seek release from this world of worry and fear. You choose.

All is about your choice and what you want in your life. Just as you are able to choose fast food that merely seems like it is nourishing, but leaves you full and wanting more, or healthy food that gives lifegiving nutrients.

I see the struggle to make the right choices. It is difficult and many are in the grip of the money-based commerce and its advertising that lures to the unhealthy. But you know what you need and those things that sustain and give you true strength and happiness. We wish that for you.

Mary

Mary's Simple Graces

All is Well, All is Well, All is Well. Say it often, "All Is Well." I know that all is well, having a higher perspective, but I also realize that when you are in the midst of chaos, crisis, or a dilemma, it is hard to know that all is well. But it always is – no matter what the situation. Even if you are dying, you will soon be in a better place. The Universe expands and always, always is going to the best of options.

If you can say, and actually believe, that all is well no matter what the circumstances, you will have an easier time in life. Write it on the wall, the mirror, in the car –All Is Well – to remind your conscious mind when you need it most what your higher self already knows. Each difficulty will pass, and the expanded you, the one who is learning, growing, and living through this experience, will *always* be well. Not only well but wiser.

Let me whisper it to you … "all is well." Let me shout it from beyond … "ALL IS WELL!!" Let your heart sing it to you into the night as you lay your head down to sleep. Before you begin to rehash the day, say and hear me say, "All Is Well."

But for now, good night my child, know you are in my bosom of safety. Even if it all looks bleak, it is not – for I am holding you even closer than usual.

Peaceful dreaming to you,
Mary

Being ill is not fun, but it is profitable, from my perspective. You spend so much time socializing, working, and being out in the world, that when illness strikes, your immune system gets to take over. It pulls all the energy from the rest of your body which makes you tired and want to lie down. This is a good way to sleep, meditate, and rest your body.

Because of illness, you finally slow down enough so we can talk to you. If you have been too busy to take the time to commune with me, sometimes your body will take over and force you to rest.

Indeed all is well with all of it. I am just sorry you have to hurt yourself, temporarily, just to talk to me. I will take you no matter how you come to me: ill, well, in a hurricane, in a car, or on your death bed. It doesn't matter how you come to me … just come.

As you understand the message of what caused this illness, you will also begin to heal. Not only will your body heal, but the underlying reason for the illness will reveal itself so it can be addressed.

Your illness is a gift so you lie down, sit down, and slow down. Loving you beyond anything you may think or feel.

Mary

You have all that you need: transportation, shelter, food, and clothing. Now is the time for you to give … give … give. Give to those who are lonely, to those who are in need of the basics, and give to those who have heartache.

Seek out the ones who are bed-ridden and need someone to bring the world to them. Search for the sad and lonely hearts. They are everywhere. You will find them if you open to their presence.

Also, balance it out with those who give to you, those who fulfill your dreams, and who are a joy to be around. They fill you with laughter and love. Then, as your cup or mug overflows, pour it out to others. It will come back to you in a multitude of ways. Even if it is not money, seek ways that you can give.

Mary

Love is all around. Do not restrict it to only the love of a partner, family, or friends. Love comes in as many forms as there are people. Find the way to love each person you encounter in your life. It will stretch you to expand your heart to include all you meet. Even the ones who frustrate or annoy you, love them more … they need it more.

Remember to love yourself, too. Say often, "I love you and I am so proud that you are providing me with a good life, good health, and good surroundings. The beauty that I bring myself is reflective of the beauty within."

Send blessings to yourself as you do your best in all situations. Encourage yourself and love what you do in life, even if it is tending the garden or sweeping the floor. Tell yourself you are doing a great job.

I am sending you love and light constantly. It fills the space where you are and spills over to those that see you on the street. Bless often all you meet. As you bless, you offer love, and you will see your own reflection becoming brighter and brighter because of these loving acts.

Love always,
Mary

Welcome Home!

You are home when you talk to me and come into my presence. You are safe and protected now. Keep this feeling and when you leave this space, this comfort zone, know that I go with you. There is NO place I am not with you. Just ask and I will make myself known to you in some way that is perfect.

The world can get a bit crazy, chaotic, and unruly. You may feel that life just isn't on your side. Look underneath for the blessing in it all. Look for the prayer that is being answered. If you look deep enough, you will see that ALL is for your highest and best good. It may seem to be changing too fast, but that is not so. It is changing at just the right speed for your growth and continual movement toward me.

What did you desire? What healing did you seek? What person are you trying to understand? What abundance are you drawing to yourself? All these and many more requests will have permanent solutions and sometimes these solutions require great changes in your life. Alterations are demanded, otherwise, your requests can not be answered.

I always answer prayer, especially the deepest and those true to who you are. So be honest about your inner most desires. I will honor those requests and give you tremendous grace and gifts.

Even as change occurs, stay close to me in praise and gratitude so you can gracefully glide through the choppy seas. I am with you ... I am *always* with you.

Mary

Read, read, and read. Read on your electronic devices, read from a paper book or newspaper, read from the sacred texts of the world. Sacred texts are those that are written with love, faith, and humor. There is Divine wisdom in most of your literature. Others are about addiction, identifying your desire for sex, money, and greed instead of deep security, love, faith, and the joy of adventure. So choose your options well. If you begin a book but find you have no good feelings about it, close it immediately. Go to another that is more suitable.

Read in the morning to set your world on the right path. Ask me what books to read and then pay attention to what I put into your life. Read at the noon hour, something that will inspire, and then at night read something soothing and quiet that will encourage restful slumber that only the dawn will awaken.

Too much entertainment and too much excitement can lead to anxiety and disharmony. News that is focused on the worst of humankind will not provide you comfort. Instead, seek that which is helpful, informative, and will actually provide solutions to your challenges.

Much is written for the service of everyone. Seek them out. I am with you, reading over your shoulder and illuminating the passages that are yours to affirm and live by. Listen for me as you read. I am there.

Mary

Mary's Simple Graces

Retreat is a joyous event. Do it often. When I talk about retreat I truly mean to get out of town, out of your daily routine, and go somewhere beautiful to refresh, renew, and rejoice. Find those places. Many have turned their lovely property into retreat centers just for the sole purpose, and soul purpose, to enhance the human condition. Please take these great opportunities to enrich your spiritual wellbeing.

Create, think, write, dream, love, meditate, pray, walk, hike, sit. Fill your life with the beauty and surroundings of nature available for you at every turn. Those that live in a large city especially need to go to the country, the beach, or mountains and retreat into nature.

Find a pot and put a flower in it, start a community garden in a vacant lot, look up more and be attentive to the birds. City dwellers can get too focused on their cityscapes and require natural surroundings that creation has to offer.

You will find that those living in a large metropolitan city will talk and prepare for their next vacation often. Once they are back from one trip, they will plan and begin to execute the next excursion. This is their way of bringing in the energy so needed for their spirit's health each day.

Please continue to dream and plan out-of-door visits as you live your urban lives. All is well, all is well.

Mary

Music is the voice of angels. You can tune into the type of music you wish to expand your energy and emotions. If you are joyful, there are sounds and harmonies that will increase and expand joyfulness. If you are depressed and wish to deepen the darkness, you also have a choice of songs that will meet you where you are and bring you closer to the abyss. Music is readily available for all emotions and experiences.

Many use music to strengthen their resolve, to motivate. Some will listen for romance and pleasure. Others will use it as noise to drown out the negative thoughts that bounce around in their minds. However you wish to use the compositions of others, it is all for you.

The best and most beneficial way to use music is to create your own. To feel an instrument vibrate with either your breath or movement – what bliss. It will radiate throughout your body and into the ethers creating a form that will drift throughout time.

Using music for praise and worship is indeed the highest form of this vibration. This sound is ever adding to the positive, blessed, and healing energy of the Earth. As you add to this pool of tune and tone, remember it is permanently imprinted into the aura of the cosmos. Be mindful of what you participate in, you will know when something you hear is touching your soul and the souls of others, it will feel as if you are dancing on air. You may even cry hearing such pure sounds.

I, at times, softly sing you to sleep at night. I am there with a soothing melody from my lips to your ears. Rest well, my child, in my song of love.

Mary

See the animals around you, find solace in them. They are carrying messages to you as well. Look at the chipmunks frolicking in the woods, tails high as they cross the road. Watch them store food in their cheeks and pack it in for the winter months.

The hummingbirds, fast and with break-neck speed, dart in and out of tree branches then gently hovering by a flower blossom, sucking the nectar from between the petals.

See the gophers, digging furiously and grabbing whole plants, dragging them back into their tunnel, nesting, eating, foraging. Moving great amounts of dirt with the finesse of a dolphin cutting through the water, the gopher swims through the soil with nose, body, and limbs.

You too go with break-neck speed through your lives only to stall at the next feeding station or coffee shop to fortify for even quicker responses and more productive days. STOP once in a while through the day and watch the critters around you. See how they work, play, and interact with the environment. Watch them sleep only to wake again with renewed enthusiasm for life. You too have a need to wake up to the newness of each dawning day.

If you are not coming out of your dreams with refreshed hope and desire for life, find your solace, find your passion, find happiness as you survive and live this life. It may take just a few minor changes to give life the accent it needs to brighten up its luster. Try it, go for it and live the life you have always dreamed of.

Always choose love,
Mary

Sometimes life is just about marking time, going though the motions, being bored and unfulfilled. This is the time that you have been praying for to get caught up on reading, writing, watching that movie you wanted to see, and to get out of the house to watch a sunset. Do not worry, life will get busy again soon, but remember this is that oasis you have wished for when you were too busy to enjoy life – so you thought.

Actually these times are productive, even though it seems nothing is getting done and you seem to be lacking passion. It will pass and that thrill of newness and enthusiasm will return. Do not fret about these times, but instead turn your attention to quieter activities that bring their own usefulness. These are "If only I had the time I would …" activities, for NOW is that time! Do those things on that list, that "when I have time, I will …" list.

Breath in this special energy and try not to distract yourself just to have something to do or be with someone just to have company. It won't work out well, this is your "me" time so embrace it, bless it, and step into it. You may have to drag yourself to initiate an activity, but you will see how much better you feel once you begin and one thing follows another smoothly.

It is a paradox isn't it, that when you have "empty" time and nothing scheduled, it sometimes feels like a void. But embrace it with gratitude and try not to get caught in inertia. We are always with you to move you through this slower time, just ask for help and we will gently nudge you forward.

Mary

Ask for what you need, if it is a pool in the summer, a heater in the winter, more nature excursions, money, health, love, or anything else that you desire – ask. If you do not ask, it cannot be given as quickly.

The Divine will answer all prayer, but it may not look as if it is acknowledged. Prayer answers may look very different than you imagined, but if you really look at what you receive, it will be perfect.

You may meet a like-minded friend that has a pool, a car that feels so good to drive that you will automatically take long road trips, you may receive a promotion at work, or a different job. Be open to receive whatever form your prayer answer comes in. It will always, ALWAYS be the highest and best of your request, if you ask for Divine intervention.

The best prayer is, of course, "May Your will be done." That will bring in so many enlightened possibilities. Then end your prayer with thanksgiving. Praise and gratitude, all is well, all is well.

Mary

Mary's Simple Graces

Walking, hiking, and running outdoors will move the body in space and bring in the opportunity to be in nature. This will blow out some stale energy and bring in health. Walk, hike, and run often, depending on what is best for your body. Riding a bicycle is helpful too, but with speed you may miss the beauty of the journey. Be sure to stop and take a break – touch a leaf, look closely at a bug, or sit on a rock. When traveling quickly to a destination, the mind will focus on the goal instead of enjoying each turn of the road. Sometimes too much is lost that only can be seen on foot.

When walking, take the unchartered path. Get off the trail a bit to see from a new perspective. See the other side of the flower, mountain, ridge, or valley. Take me with you, I will be there for you whenever you wish me to come along. I have much to show you in this vast creation.

Mary

"My soul proclaims the Greatness of the Divine"

So true and you too can continually proclaim the Greatness of the Divine. My soul loves God and there is no greater joy than to extol the Creator. When I, as a woman said those words, I thought there was no greater joy until I passed through the veil of death and now live closer to the Divine then ever before.

I stand with the angels rejoicing the goodness, power, and mercy of God. If I could give you a glimpse of what is to come upon your transition into glory, you would weep that you were not here now. No worry though, you will all be here soon enough, you will *all* come home to the bosom of the Divine.

Proclaim the greatness of God in your lives. Use your mouths, your words to tell each other what miracles and synchronicities have happened in your life. It will uplift and encourage those you know. A story of a miracle told to another will bring an awe-filled feeling into someone else's life. It will magnify the original touch of Divine Grace into the world.

Little daily stories passed on, bring hope and reminds us of great power when all seems so powerless. When life and purpose seem lost or empty, alone or desperate, hearing such a tale of hope opens a door to the light of God.

Speak often, let your soul soar and share the spark of life. Put that praise of grace into words and expand it by sharing it with those around you.

Loving you,
Mary

Mary's Simple Graces

"My spirit rejoices in God my Savior"

Yes, God is my Savior, saving me from so many dark days and moments. I would just keep walking, filled with fear and then an angel would appear in some form. It could be a smile from a stranger, a bird lighting next to me, a feather, a sunset, an encouragement from a friend or relative, a passage from scripture, an inner voice of love, or a feeling of Divine presence. Then I was saved time and time again.

My spirit-breath breathes the joyous song to God. I open my arms upward to send thanksgiving, love, and joy. I receive so much more than I am capable of holding as the Divine floods my spirit with goodness and love. I have to let it out in graces to you because I am bursting with Holy Love.

Sacred scripture holds so much power that when I partook of a daily reading, contemplation, and meditation while on earth, I would feel Divine grace. I love the Divine more than a husband. Joseph knew this and being a Holy man himself, he loved the Lord as his own too. We were very happy together in our chosen mission to care for our son, Jesus, but to also love and commune with the Divine in our relationship, our marriage was blessed. I was certainly blessed amongst women.

Mary

Mary's Simple Graces

"God has looked with favor on this lowly servant."

When the Angel Gabriel came to tell me about my chosen mission and the importance of the child I was to bear, at first I was afraid. I certainly didn't feel worthy but then knew somewhere deep in my heart the angels and God would help me. I would indeed be blessed and that I would be able to do whatever I was asked to do with this much Divine assistance and love.

I couldn't believe the overwhelming joy I felt. Once the angel left I had to go tell Elizabeth of my visitation and conception. There was a spirit living in me that was, indeed, miraculous and sacred. I felt that immediately. It was so powerful that no mother could ever believe that there wasn't a holy soul within her body. I knew the moment Jesus was conceived. I lived with this power and glory for those many months. My body was truly blessed.

Sending all mothers my love, strength, and grace.
Mary

The POWER of God is so tremendous that nothing, NOTHING can stand against it. Look at a hurricane, a storm, the stars, moon, or sun. All have natural power, but the Divine who created all this is so powerful that we are just unable to grasp the enormity of that much strength.

Why worry, fret, or fear? Pray to the One who has ALL power and might, the energy is immense. This One loves you and wants to give you everything possible, like a parent to a child, is always present. There is no negativity, no evil, no disease, nor circumstance that cannot be at least bettered, but totally changed with the touch of the Divine.

As the angel Gabriel told me, "Nothing is impossible for God." Remember that when you think there is no hope, no possible way something could change. Pray to the One who loves you most. See how this One will perform miracles to right a wrong and will cure an illness in mind, body, and spirit. Just give it to God.

Mary

Mary's Simple Graces

You are exactly where you are supposed to be at this time. If you were to be somewhere else, you would be there. I would have moved you to your new path and opened up new vistas for you. But not right now. There is still much to learn from where you are. Once you have learned and attained all the gifts I have to offer you, then a move will be eminent and with great ease.

So look where you are and what needs to be done. What is that nagging in your inner world that says you are to do something? Do it now or ask for help to get it done. You are only delaying your own progress. No one else will be affected as much as you are in your procrastination. We wait for you to finish so you can go into your new destiny.

Remember, this was your dream at one time. So live it and enjoy it as you are also building your new reality in your consciousness. As in building a foundation of a house, you have to dig the hole, lay the slab, and build the walls before you can sleep in the bedroom. If we hurry the process, you will have a unstable base.

While you are laying brick and pouring cement, it is good to imagine when all is complete, but if you work with impatience and frustration that it is taking so long, that will only put an unkind energy into your framework.

Labor always with love, prayer, laughter, and delight from your day's work. All is perfect Divine timing. All is, indeed, well, all is, indeed, well.

Mary

Mary's Simple Graces

At the end of the day, rest, and appreciate the beauty around you. Night is coming. It is a time to be with friends and family to talk about the events of the day. It is also a time to be quiet, to do those things that hadn't been done because of prior busyness. Read, talk, walk, and contemplate. Feel the coolness of the nightfall. Hear the quieting of the birds and the increased activity of the creatures of the night – the bats, the crickets, the lightening bugs.

Feel yourself embrace the restful and peacefulness of twilight. Play an instrument, a lullaby, a ballad, a hymn. Praise God for a day well done and be grateful for purposeful work, loving relations, food, and drink.

It is time to rest and appreciate. Be in this time and all will take care of itself in the morn. You will be ready for it then, at the dawn of a new and refreshed day. But not tonight, sleep well, dream peaceful, and release.

Goodnight,
Mary

Find your sacred place, whether it be a church, temple, synagogue, rushing river, beach, bench, or by a window in your home. I am there. Come often to speak with me and be in my presence. I am waiting for you whenever and wherever you make the time for me.

Have several places where you meet me; as long as it is quiet and lovely. That is how I am. Be open to receive healing, guidance, and love at those times. I am sitting right next to you, in front of you, or walking with you on your journey.

Make a place for me in your heart and in your home. That will add to the amount of time you will spend with me. I am here for you. Have an altar, a statue, a candle, something that lets me know you are calling. When I feel you drawing near and hear your heart yearning for me, I will be there.

Always,
Mary

Mary's Simple Graces

Look up to the sky, the stars, the moon, the clouds; the Universe and Creation is vast. Your little thoughts and designs will be dwarfed by just remembering your place in the cosmos. See what you deal with daily from a higher perspective. For example, from the moon, the closest heavenly body, and can you see what freedom you can create out of your current constrained thinking? Breathe in this freedom, infinite possibilities, more than you can even know while stuck in this downward vision.

As you raise your eyes and head upward, the energy of your being and whatever situation you find yourself, will dwindle into its true importance. There is so much more beyond this limited view.

All of life is in a tiny leaf, in a raindrop, a snowflake, or grain of sand. But somehow this small being can forget the larger picture and that its true place is more than on a tree, in a storm, on a snow covered mountain, or a long expanse of a beach. Each wave carries a piece of the ocean, each ocean carries the totality of the seas, and all water is connected even if it is vapor, steam, dew, mist, ice, or snow. All is connected to the greater good. Big and small, mini and macro – All is One.

Mary

It is safe in this world and particularly where you are. Most of your night terrors are only the fears of the mind making up spooky stories. You are safe and sound in your world. When you are in trouble, you will have a very different feeling about it. It will not be in your mind, it will be in your solar plexus. You will have what you call a "gut feeling" and this will be as if a siren is going off in the base and core of your being.

You have had this warning system go off in the past. Think of those times and then compare that with what you are feeling now. It is completely different. It is your mind is scaring you. Allow the mind to calm down. Be peaceful, hear my words that all is well and that you are safe. No longer live on the defensive, looking out for any and all danger that you will meet during the day.

If you were in the armed forces, law enforcement, or careers where danger is indeed faced everyday, there is a knowing among those professionals of what "real" danger feels like. They can sense it deep inside. It is not something they can pass over easily. It is a very real sensation that is different from any other.

So Dear Ones, rest assured, sleep peacefully, and know your Guardian Angel and I are watching over you today and tonight. Sleep well, all is well, we send you blessings and sweet thoughts.

Mary

As you go outside and spend more time in nature, you will see how much your creativity, opportunities, and life will expand and be drawn to you. If you are cooped up in your home, or too focused on your work, your world will literally become smaller and less "good fortune" and synchronicity will occur. This constrained energy is blocking off all that is trying to come and assist you. Once you go on a much needed vacation, take a walk, or engage in a fun activity, the world will look very different, bigger, and your spirit will use this time to offer you expanded ideas and circumstances.

Have you ever been on a holiday when you felt as if you could no longer stand your job and you began to plan a change of career, or move to a different part of the world? You have literally broken from the stagnation you have created. Then from a higher perspective of what is possible for you, you look at your life. Insights happened because you were traveling, out of doors, and outside of your comfort zone long enough to allow in a new possibility.

Many people will go on trip and move to where they vacationed. It was beautiful or offered so much more than what they had in their old home town that they couldn't bear to go back to the dull, lifeless existence. They had to take the leap into their new world and life. They followed their bliss!

You, too, can do that every single day of your life. Allow your mind to stay open to newness, to imagine what could be possible, where would you live, what would your lifestyle be, who would you be with? Stay open to fresh ideas, see what people are doing that expands their lives and learn from them.

Keep your thoughts a bit above the physical plane and your

mundane activities so you are always present to see the higher view each and every day. That will keep you bright, open for change, and young in your hearts and souls.

Mary

Playing games, participating in sports, and exercising the body energizes not only the body but focuses your thoughts and frees the spirit. Movement will be the life blood. Even if you have a disability that does not allow you to play in certain ways, everything can be modified. Watch others follow their play-hearts and physical abilities.

Some will only engage in activities where there is competition, others will want to just have some fun. Either way, strive to be the best you can be without placing high expectations upon your performance. Too high of expectations may lead to limited exaltation and dissatisfaction for not reaching your perfectionist ideals.

Just have a bit of fun, laugh, cheer, and be excited for the opportunity to be a team, an athlete, and the star of your own championship.

Love always,
Mary

Mary's Simple Graces

Always choose love. No matter the situation or conflict. What is the loving decision at this point? Respond, do not react. Soften your stomach, eyes, and open your heart to expand and embrace this new level of love. It will be so worth it. You will greatly benefit from choosing this loving and higher path.

Fear is your worst enemy. No other will kill you or your joy faster. Faith will change fear into a joyful reliance and trust in the Divine. The Universe is loving, generous, and always expanding to new opportunities for love and faith.

You have asked to be here to learn these most important lessons on this physical plane. I know it is hard, harder than diamonds, but it can be done and we will help you each step of the way.

It is easy to love those who are nice, kind, and generous. It is difficult to shift to love when you are fearful and angry. But just as turning the channel on a radio or TV, turn to the love and faith channel within yourself. Pause and ask for help. We will always provide you with the love and faith alternative. It is our job to be of such service. We love it when we see you struggle and then choose a different, more loving response.

Just ask, I am always here for you. Have the courage to take this step each and every time to find a more loving and faithful way in the world. Walk away from your fear and hatred. It does not serve you in any way. Just turn your face to me, to God, and to the angels. We will embrace and teach you this humble, loving, and trusting way.

All is well, all is well – with love and faith – all is well,
Mary

Mary's Prayers

Behold my children, this is a time of great growth and you may require a bit of help from the Divine and I. Please receive these prayer offerings as a beginning to, or a continuation of, your prayer life.

Many Blessings are yours,
Mary

Most Holy God, Creator of the Universe, beat of my heart and breath of my body.

May Your Will be done in our country, the Earth, and the Universe, but especially in our lives as we walk with You.

Teach me to be generous in words, actions, and deeds with love and kindness.

Help me to forgive those who have harm in their intent and hatred in their minds.

Make me the one who chooses love and shows a better way of being.

Give me strength to oppose the wrongs and support the loving way and those who walk in that path.

Open a door that will let the light of You into the darkest of places and protect me as I forge forward to do Your Will.

Amen

Dearest Beloved Divine,

Come to me now and show me the way out of this fear and loneliness. Guide me back to You and Your life giving light. May I feel Your presence in my awakening and in my evening time with You. Walk with me, be at my side, in front and around me at all times with Your strong force of Love. May Your love that embodies me touch all those that I encounter in my day.

I thank you with great gratitude and thanksgiving.

Amen

Loving Mary, Mother of us all,

Be with us in this time of great unrest. Be with us politically, spiritually, and with our warring factions. Bring your loving grace, generosity, and forgiveness into our prayers, our words, and our actions today. Be with those who oppose us and guide us with open communication of understanding of our many differences and diversity. Please bless us in our dealings to find a way which is the highest and best for all.

Amen

Thank you, Mary, for loving me right where I am in this moment – with all my goodness and my faults. You have taught me that I am loved unconditionally, and how that lovingkindness has changed me. Please help me to give to my fellow travelers on this road of life that same unconditional love and understanding as we all grow into being our Higher selves – mistakes and all. Be with me as I pray for your intercession into my thoughts, judgements, and sentencing of those who differ from me. Open my heart, mind, and spirit to offer the flower of peace to all and add a bit more generosity and forgiveness to this world.

With you as my guide.

Amen

About the Author

Kermie Wohlenhaus, Ph.D. is an author, angelologist, and clairvoyant. She teaches classes, workshops, and offers presentations nationally. Kermie is popular in live performance, with radio and TV audiences for her humor and accurate intuitive messages and knowledge.

Kermie Wohlenhaus, Ph.D. has also authored:

How to Talk and Actually Listen to Your Guardian Angel which is available in Spanish, French, German, and Dutch.

The award-winning *Shopping with the Virgin Mary*

Dr. Wohlenhaus has also annotated foundation texts for the field of Angelology, such as the *Angels in Sacred Texts* series which includes:
The Complete Reference to Angels in The Bible
A Quick Reference Guide to Angels in The Bible
The Complete Reference to Angels in The Book of Mormon
The Complete Reference to Angels in The Koran (Qu'ran)

She is currently living in Tucson, Arizona.

For further information: www.KermieWohlenhaus.com

www.ingramcontent.com/pod-product-compliance
Lightning Source LLC
Chambersburg PA
CBHW060834110426
R18122100001BA/R181221PG42736CBX00025BA/23